Reading and Writing
Non-Fiction

Tim Ayres and John Dayus

Heinemann Educational Publishers
Halley Court, Jordan Hill, Oxford, OX2 8EJ
a division of Reed Educational and Professional Publishing Ltd
Heinemann is a registered trademark of Reed Educational and Professional Publishing Ltd
OXFORD MELBOURNE AUCKLAND
JOHANNESBURG BLANTYRE GABORONE
IBADAN PORTSMOUTH NH (USA) CHICAGO

© Tim Ayres and John Dayus, 2000

First published 2000

ISBN 0 435 10579 5

04 03 02 01 00

10 9 8 7 6 5 4 3 2 1

Designed and typeset by Gecko Ltd Bicester Oxon UK

Illustrated by Original Illustrations © Heinemann Educational Publishers. 2000; Chris Brown: pages 9, 15, 80, 81; Gecko DTP: page 27; Tim Davies: pages 40, 66, 88; Belinda Evans: page 57; Gary Wing: page 63; Chris Long: page 68; Beccy Blake: page 72; Andrew Quelch: page 78; Abigail Conway: page 110; Nick Schon: page 128;

Cover design by JPH Design + Illustration

Printed and bound in Spain by Mateu Cromo

Acknowledgements
The authors and publishers would like to thank the following for permission to use copyright material:

Ernie Pyle: 'The Ocean was Infested with Ships', 'A Surge of Doom-like Sound' and 'Debris and Utter Silence', reproduced by permission of Britannica Online, pp 16-20; extracts from *The Kingfisher Children's Encyclopaedia* ed John Paton, © Larousse Kingfisher Chambers Inc, pp30-31; 'Ancient Greece: Sparta' by Richard Law from the website of Washington State University, reproduced by permission of Washington State University, p37; extracts from 'Horrible Histories' and 'Horrible Science' © Scholastic Ltd, pp38 and 50-51; 'Toyota Avensis' from Which Online, reproduced by permission of WHICH, p42; extracts from *Eyewitness Science Guides: How Things Work* by Neil Ardley, © Dorling Kindersley, pp48-49 and 54; 'Ebeneezer's Guide to Colds and Flu' reproduced by permission of Propriety Association of Great Britain, p53; extract from *Walking with Dinosaurs* by Tim Haines, reproduced with the permission of BBC Worldwide Ltd, © Tim Haines 1999, pp 60-61; 'Snow Shelters' from *Outdoor Survival Guide* by Hugh McManners, © Dorling Kindersley, p75; 'Sun Dried Tomato Omelette' from *Sainsbury's Quick and Easy Vegetarian Meals for Students* by Rose Elliot, reproduced by permission of HarperCollins Publishers Ltd, p76; 'Travelling in Barbados' from *Barbados Mini Rough Guide* by Adam Vaitlingham, © Rough Guides, p79; 'Back Country Food and Water' by Teri Matthews from twsnet.com, reproduced by permission of twsnet.com, pp80-81; 'Problem Page' from *Live and Kicking Magazine*, reproduced by permission of TOTP and L&K magazines, p82; 'Problem Page' from Star Girl Magazine, reproduced by permission of Star Girl Magazine, p83; 'Baby for Adoption' leaflet reproduced by permission of the Whale and Dolphin Conservation Society, p90; advertisement for Panasonic mobile phone reproduced by permission of Panasonic and the photographer Fleur Olby, p90; 'Birmingham Appeal' leaflet reproduced by permission of the Imperial Cancer Research Fund, p91; 'Downhill Mountain Biking for Playstation' reproduced by permission of Codemasters, p91; 'The Truth Zone' by Matthew Hinkley from *The Daily Mail* 17/1/00, reproduced by permission of Atlantic Syndication Partners, p96; 'Prime Real Estate on the Moon' from explorezone.com, reproduced by permission of explorezone.com, p104.

Whilst every effort has been made to locate the owners of copyright, in some cases this has been unsuccessful. The publishers apologise for any omission of original sources and will be pleased to make the necessary arrangements at the first opportunity.

The authors and publishers would like to thank the following for permission to use photographs:

Peter Goodfellow, p12; Corbis, p16; Corbis, p16; B.H.Ward & K.C.Ward/Corbis, p18; Bettmann/Corbis, p19; Corbis, p21; Ric Ergenbright/Corbis, p22; Photodisc, p29; Photodisc, p39; Photodisc, p39; Bettmann/Corbis, p43; Galen Rowell/Corbis, p60; Photodisc, p61; HarperCollins/David Armstrong, p76; Photodisc, p79; Lee Snider/Corbis, p109; Photodisc, p117; Photodisc, p118.

Tel: 01865 888058   www.heinemann.co.uk

Introduction

Welcome to **Reading and Writing Non-Fiction**.

When we are young children, we first start to hear fiction stories from our parents. We are told fairy stories. We learn the value of such stories, and very soon we probably begin to write our own stories. For most of us, if we are asked to write a story, we can do it without too much difficulty because we are familiar with the style and structure of such writing. Similarly, reading fiction doesn't usually pose too many problems. We can follow the action with relative ease, and understand the story that the author is unfolding for us.

One reason for this is that narrative writing is based upon a 'what happens next' structure. On the whole, fiction writers stick to the known formula: a story must have a beginning, a middle and an end.

Non-fiction writing is structured rather differently. For instance, if an essay starts with: 'I believe that in the twenty-first century, schools will no longer be needed', then what follows does not answer the 'what happens next' question. Rather, the questions might be:

- Why not?
- What evidence do you have to support this idea?
- What would replace schools?
- How would this work?

In this book, you will be studying how authors structure non-fiction writing, and how the language that they use is affected by the type of non-fiction that they are dealing with. You will also be given many opportunities to develop your own writing in the different genres: description, explanation, information, advice, persuasion and argument.

You will also be given opportunities to study pupils' writing, and apply GCSE criteria to the writing, so you can develop a clear understanding of the demands of GCSE.

We hope that you will find this book to be helpful as you prepare for GCSE English.

Equally importantly, we hope you enjoy your exploration of non-fiction writing.

Tim Ayres and John Dayus

Contents

Introduction

Unit 1 Description

When you think of a description, you probably think of it in the context of narrative writing. We all understand that as writers, we must help the reader to engage with the scene and the characters, so we use description to bring characters to life, and to paint a picture of the scene.

However, description is very important in many different types of speech and writing. For instance, consider the following:

- a description of a football match by a radio commentator
- a description of a suspect in a robbery
- a description of the symptoms of an illness
- a description of a missing pet
- a description of a piece of jewellery on a TV shopping channel
- a description of a city in a guide book.

In each case, the *audience* for the description is different; also, the *purpose* of the writing is different in each case. Therefore, *the way in which description is used* will also differ.

TASK 1

In pairs, discuss the above contexts for descriptions. In each case, try to agree about exactly who the **audience** is, what the **purpose** of the writing is, and finally, what **effect on the writing** these two factors will have.

Make a table of your findings, under the headings above.

TASK 2

Suggest seven more examples of writing which make use of description for different purposes. Once more, list your suggestions in the form of a table, using the same headings that you used in Task 1.

By now, you should have some idea of the *scope* for writing descriptions.

In this unit, you will be:
- studying how the intended purpose of the description will have an effect on how description is used, and trying to understand and explain the differences you see in descriptions
- demonstrating your understanding of description in the context of non-fiction in your own writing.

Different purposes for writing a description

When considering the third description on page 7 (a description of the symptoms of an illness), it was clear that it was very important for the patient to be as accurate as possible in their description, so that the doctor could make a correct diagnosis.

In the descriptions below, the authors are also trying to record their experiences accurately, in order to demonstrate the authenticity of their UFO sightings.

The first extract describes triangular UFOs seen above Eastlake in Ohio in 1988. The sighting was made by a woman who identified herself only as 'S.B.'

The second extract reports a sighting by a man called A. C. Urie who operated a trout farm in Idaho, and dates from August 1947.

Read the descriptions carefully, and then complete the task which follows.

Triangular UFOs above Eastlake, Ohio, USA, 1988

It was a clear, crisp night. The stars were clearly visible, especially to the north over the lake where there are no city lights. Venus and Jupiter were bright and in close proximity to each other in the western sky. At about 6:30 P.M., S.B. and her children were driving home to Eastlake along the lake shore when they observed a large blimp-like object with lights at each end, hovering over the lake and rocking up and down like a 'teeter totter.'

One light was brighter than the other and was strobing. On arriving home, she asked her husband to accompany her to the beach about 200 yards north for a closer view of the object which she described as 'larger than a football field at arm's length.'

She and her husband walked onto the beach. The noiseless object was gun metal gray and seemed to cause the ice on the lake to rumble and crack loudly in an unusual way which frightened her.

The object revolved slowly about 90 degrees, coming almost overhead (about 1/4 mile high) and pointing its 'front' end down toward them. The object began to descend and the witnesses observed it to have red and blue blinking lights. It emitted 5 or 6 noiseless, intensely bright yellow triangular lights from its side. Mr. B. noticed a brighter light at the apex of the triangles. They intermittently hovered around the larger object, darted and zig-zagged into the night sky at velocities far in excess of known aircraft.

Mr. B. stated the noiseless triangular objects were smaller than a one-seater Cessna aircraft and travelled 50 mile stretches low over the ice in the 'snap of a finger.'

The triangles continued to fly off at high speed northward over the lake and eastward toward the Power Plant. About an hour later, they returned one at a time into the large ship, which then landed on the ice. Several multi-colored lights now came on for about 5 minutes on the bottom of the object 'in a wave like a movie theater sign.' When these went off, the ice stopped making noise and everything became 'dead silent.'

Flying saucers over Idaho, USA, 1947

Urie explained that the incident occurred while the two boys were coming across the river from the north side in a boat. He had become concerned about what was delaying them and had walked down toward the river to see if they were all right.

'I had a side view at a distance of about 300 feet and almost on a level with the thing,' Urie continued. 'Two of my boys, Keith and Billy, were below me and they also saw it at about a 45-degree angle. They both got a bottom and a side view, and we were all looking at it from the south side of the canyon … It was all one color, sort of a light sky blue with a red tubular fiery glow at the side of the top, or hood,' Urie continued. 'The canyon floor is rough at that particular point and it rode up and down over the hills and hollows at a speed indicating some type of control faster than the reflexes of man. It is my opinion that it is guided by instruments and must be powered by atomic energy as it made very little noise, just a s-w-i-s-h as it passed by.'

Urie described the size as about 20 feet long by 10 feet high and 10 feet wide, giving it an oblong shape. It might be described as looking like an inverted pie plate or broad-brimmed straw hat that had been compressed from two sides.

As it went over Urie's house, the poplar trees over which it passed did not just bend with the wind as if a plane had gone by, but in Urie's words, 'spun around on top as if they were in a vacuum.'

TASK 3

Answer these questions for each of the passages. You might find it helpful to make a table like the one below for each of the descriptions, or use the tables provided in the TRF.

a) The authors describe the *setting* for the sighting.
- How do they describe it?
- Why do they do so?

b) Although these are pieces of non-fiction writing, the authors often use *imagery* in order to give the reader a clear idea of what they saw.
- Where do they do this?
- How does the imagery help the reader to form a picture of what was seen?

c) The authors not only recorded what was *seen*, but also what was *heard* by the witnesses.
- Where do the authors draw attention to the sounds?
- What is the effect of this?

d) How do the authors draw attention to *light* and *colour* in their descriptions?

Triangular UFOs above Eastlake, Ohio, USA, 1988	
a) Why does the author describe the setting? How does he describe it?	b) Where does the author use imagery? How does it help the reader to form a picture of what was seen?
c) Where does the author draw attention to sounds? What is the effect of this?	d) How does the author draw attention to light and colour in the description?

Over the last three pages, you have looked at descriptions that have been written to describe apparently real events. As you have seen, the authors were trying to demonstrate the authenticity of the sightings by making very specific, realistic comparisons, and by being very precise when describing such things as settings and sounds.

One thing that should have become clear is that the writers were not setting out to entertain the reader, as do writers of narratives (stories). Indeed, if they had used language to entertain, it would almost certainly have had the effect of making readers doubt their integrity.

So it would be useful to investigate exactly what the differences are between descriptions in narratives and descriptions in other, non-narrative contexts. In order to do this, you are going to compare the accounts you have just read with an extract from a book called *The War of the Worlds*, written in 1898 by H. G. Wells.

Although the book was fictional, the writer deliberately wrote it in a 'semi-documentary' style in order to make the book 'realistic'. The opening of the second chapter has been printed below. Read it, and then complete the task which follows.

The War of the Worlds, 1898

Then came the night of the first falling star. It was seen early in the morning, rushing over Winchester eastward, a line of flame high in the atmosphere. Hundreds must have seen it, and taken it for an ordinary falling star. Albin described it as leaving a greenish streak behind it that glowed for some seconds. Denning, our greatest authority on meteorites, stated that the height of its first appearance was about ninety or one hundred miles. It seemed to him that it fell to earth about one hundred miles east of him.

I was at home at that hour and writing in my study; and although my French windows face towards Ottershaw and the blind was up (for I loved in those days to look up at the night sky), I saw nothing of it. Yet this strangest of all things that ever came to earth from outer space must have fallen while I was sitting there, visible to me had I only looked up as it passed. Some of those who saw its flight say it travelled with a hissing sound. I myself heard nothing of that. Many people in Berkshire, Surrey, and Middlesex must have seen the fall of it, and, at most, have thought that another meteorite had descended. No one seems to have troubled to look for the fallen mass that night.

But very early in the morning poor Ogilvy, who had seen the shooting star and who was persuaded that a meteorite lay somewhere on the common between Horsell, Ottershaw, and Woking, rose early with the idea of finding it. Find it he did, soon after dawn, and not far from the sand pits. An enormous hole had been made by the impact of the projectile, and the sand and gravel had been flung violently in every direction over the heath, forming heaps visible a mile and a half away. The heather was on fire eastward, and a thin blue smoke rose against the dawn.

The Thing itself lay almost entirely buried in sand, amidst the scattered splinters of a fir tree it had shivered to fragments in its descent. The uncovered part had the appearance of a huge cylinder, caked over and its outline softened by a thick scaly dun-coloured incrustation. It had a diameter of about thirty yards. He approached the mass, surprised at the size and more so at the shape, since most meteorites are rounded more or less completely. It was, however, still so hot from its flight through the air as to forbid his near approach. A stirring noise within its cylinder he ascribed to the unequal cooling of its surface; for at that time it had not occurred to him that it might be hollow.

He remained standing at the edge of the pit that the Thing had made for itself, staring at its strange appearance, astonished chiefly at its unusual shape and colour, and dimly perceiving even then some evidence of design in its arrival. The early morning was wonderfully still, and the sun, just clearing the pine trees towards Weybridge, was already warm. He did not remember hearing any birds that morning, there was certainly no breeze stirring, and the only sounds were the faint movements from within the cindery cylinder. He was all alone on the common.

Then suddenly he noticed with a start that some of the grey clinker, the ashy incrustation that covered the meteorite, was falling off the circular edge of the end. It was dropping off in flakes and raining down upon the sand. A large piece suddenly came off and fell with a sharp noise that brought his heart into his mouth.

The War of the Worlds by H.G. Wells

TASK 4

Draw a table like the one below.

In the first column, quote passages where the author has tried to write with a documentary style, his language reflecting a sense of realism. Add your own comments on the passages you quote.

In the second column, give examples where the author has tended to allow the 'narrative' or 'fictional' element of his descriptions to emerge. Add your own comments again. You might want to make comparisons with the descriptions of the UFO sightings in this column.

An example of each style has been done for you.

Remember, H. G. Wells was aiming to write in a semi-documentary style, in other words, half in the style of a documentary, and by implication (as this is a novel) half in a narrative style. This exercise should show if he was successful in achieving his aim.

Documentary style	Fictional style
1. 'Denning, our greatest authority … It seemed to him that it fell to earth about one hundred miles east of him.' Seems to be a plain, factual statement. No attempt to use language to excite the reader.	1. 'The early morning was wonderfully still, and the sun, just clearing the pine trees towards Weybridge, was already warm.' In the statements of the UFO witnesses, any description of the weather was merely to demonstrate that the night was clear and they therefore could not have been mistaken in what they saw. Here, there is a clear intention to engage the reader and help them to develop a visual picture of the scene.
2.	2.

TASK 5

Write about 350–400 words explaining the differences between the narrative and non-narrative descriptions which you have seen in this unit so far. Use the work that you have completed for Tasks 3 and 4 to support your observations.

In the final piece of work in this section, you will be demonstrating your understanding of the difference between narrative and non-narrative descriptions by writing two short pieces in different styles.

On 8 December 1996, Maria Elisa de Barros, Sergel Sanchez and Karen Lustrup entered 'Area 51', a wide-ranging tract of restricted US Government land about two hours from Las Vegas in the Nevada Desert. The land contains a secret US Air Force base.

The weather was 'good and clear' except for a cloud over the base, which they estimated to be about 25–40 metres up, and 15–20 metres tall. The diameter of the cloud was estimated at approximately one kilometre.

They claimed to have seen a UFO, and attempted to video it. They had two camcorders, but both of them failed to record the pictures. However, the sound did record, and printed below and opposite is a transcript of the recording.

Read it carefully, and then complete the task which follows.

(Sergel is stressed up, excitement, and fear)

K: Relax, this is an 'ordinary road', be calm … it'll be … – oh my god, what is that …? It's, oh my god … it's hovering …

S: It's going up and down …

K: Stand still … My god … look at it … it's … beautiful!

S & K: Marialisa, you got to get out here.

S: Oh Ma … hurry! Close the car door!

K: The camera is not picking up …

S: Come on camera … come on, come on …

M: What?

S: Look down the road. Tell me what you see and say we're not nuts. It's no car …

K: Nope, it's hovering over the road … bouncing … It came out of that mountain … It came down from the mountain, went to the left then the right – and now it's here …

M: I see it … Look at it … it's not on the ground … *(Size of a Volkswagen – bright orange)* – it's hovering!

S: Look at the contours … do you see that Marialisa?

K: There it goes, to the left, there it goes to the right … oooops, it shot something!, wait …

K: It's playing

S: It's neat!

S: Down

K: Down

S: Left …

K: Left …

BOTH: Round ... round ... up ... up!

K: Oh wow, see it's moving around ... it's going back and forth.

S: Right there ...

S: Dimming down ...

K: Dimming more ... Flash bright! Dimming ...

S: Gone ... It's gone.

K: There's something over there, flashes behind the cloud ... inside the cloud. It's just a tiny little cloud ... (*not the big circular cloud*)

S: What was that?

K: It was a flash of yellow light on the fender. Where did it come from ...?

K: Ohhhh, look it, look it ... ahhhh, look it – it's soooo beautiful, Marialisa look out the window ... right, right ... shoot, the camera's not getting it ... wowww, reappeared, –

S: Back/forth ... look at it move ...

K: Lights ... yes ... dim ...

BOTH: Wooowww, go, go, go! Look at it gooooo!

K: Look at it, look at it, straight ... up to the left, up to the left, straight up, up, ... hover, right, hover, hover, right ...

BOTH: Up, up ... it's the same one, the same one playing on the road ...

K: Ohhhhhh wowww!

S: Wowww, look at it play ...!

K: Up, sometimes the lights go off, there it is, going off, on, there it is ...

S: It's got a brother, right up there on the range ...

K: I can't believe we're seeing this!

S: I can't believe we're doing this ...

TASK 6

You are going to write two short descriptive pieces, each of about 300 words, based on the taped transcript above.

a) The first piece should be written in the style of a chapter from a novel, where your aim is to use description to engage and entertain your reader.

b) In the second piece, you are writing a report for *UFO Magazine*, and are using description to demonstrate the authenticity of the sighting.

Recording events

In this section, you will be looking at how descriptions can be used to record events. For instance, whenever there are significant news events – extreme weather conditions, protest marches, appearances by famous personalities and so on, news agencies immediately send out reporters. It is their job to describe the scene – to record what happens as well as attempting to convey its atmosphere.

In order to study how writers do this, we will be looking particularly at the work of the American writer Ernie Pyle (right), a winner of the Pulitzer Prize, who reported on the Normandy Landings towards the end of the Second World War.

Read his report of the invasion below, and then answer the questions which follow.

The Ocean was Infested with Ships

NORMANDY BEACHHEAD, *June 15, 1944* – The ship on which I rode to the invasion of the Continent brought certain components of the second wave of assault troops. We arrived in the congested waters of the beachhead shortly after dawn on D-One Day.

As we came down, the English Channel was crammed with forces going both ways, and as I write it still is. Minesweepers had swept wide channels for us, all the way from England to France. These were marked with buoys. Each channel was miles wide.

We surely saw there before us more ships than any human had ever seen before at one glance. And going north were other vast convoys, some composed of fast liners speeding back to England for new loads of troops and equipment.

As far as you could see in every direction, the ocean was infested with ships. There must have been every type of ocean-going vessel in the world. I even thought I saw a paddle-wheel steamer in the distance, but that was probably an illusion.

There were battleships and all other kinds of warships clear down to patrol boats. There were great fleets of Liberty ships. There were fleets of luxury liners turned into troop transports, and fleets of big landing craft and tank carriers and tankers. And in and out through it all were nondescript ships – converted yachts, riverboats, tugs, and barges.

The best way I can describe this vast armada and the frantic urgency of the traffic is to suggest that you visualize New York Harbour on its busiest day of the year and then just enlarge that scene until it takes in all the ocean the human eye can reach, clear around the horizon. And over the horizon there are dozens of times that many.

We were not able to go ashore immediately after arriving off the invasion coast amidst the great pool of ships in what was known as the 'transport area.'

Here we were in a front-row seat at a great military epic. Shells from battleships were whamming over our heads, and occasionally a dead man floated face downward past us. Hundreds and hundreds of ships laden with death milled around us. We could stand at the rail and see both our shells and German shells exploding on the beaches, where struggling men were leaping ashore, desperately hauling guns and equipment in through the water.

We were in the very vortex of the war – and yet, as we sat there waiting, Lt. Chuck Conick and I played gin rummy in the wardroom and Bing Crosby sang 'Sweet Leilani' over the ship's phonograph.*

Angry shells hitting near us would make heavy thuds as the concussion carried through the water and struck the hull of our ship. But in our wardroom men in gas-impregnated uniforms and wearing lifebelts sat reading *Life* and listening to the BBC telling us how the war before our eyes was going.

But it wasn't like that ashore. No, it wasn't like that ashore.

phonograph – record player

TASK 7

a) Who do you think was the *audience* for Ernie Pyle's report? What was his *purpose* in writing the report?

b) Pupils are often told not to start a sentence with 'And' or 'But', yet Ernie Pyle frequently does so. Why does he do this? What effect does it have on the picture he is trying to convey?

c) How do the actions of the men as they wait to disembark contrast with what is going on around them? Why do you think the author drew attention to this?

d) How does the author gradually build up a picture of the *vastness* of the operation? Refer closely to the passage to support your explanation. You should aim to write between 250 and 300 words.

In your explanation, you should discuss:
- individual words   e.g. 'crammed'
- imagery   e.g. what is the effect of imagery such as 'Here we were in a front-row seat at a great military epic'?
- sentence structure   see question **b)**
- use of repetition   e.g. repetition of 'There were …' in the fifth paragraph.

As you have learned, it is important when writing descriptions to describe sounds as well as what a place looks like. This makes a scene much more vivid to the reader. For instance, central to the UFO witnesses' accounts of sightings are the sounds made by the UFOs.

In Ernie Pyle's report below, the importance of sound is clearly suggested by the title of the piece: 'A Surge of Doom-like Sound'. He does not describe only the sounds of the invasion; as you will see, he also describes what he *saw* in considerable detail. However, it is clear that his description of the intense *noise* of the battle is central to his report, and essential to his intention to convey the atmosphere of the battle.

TASK 8

a) Read the passage below, and write down all the references to sounds in the passage. Make sure you write them down in the order in which they occur.

b) Explain how Ernie Pyle's description of the noise changes and develops as you move through the report. What do you think is the effect of these changes? Write about 60 words.

A Surge of Doom-like Sound

IN NORMANDY, *August 8, 1944* – Our front lines were marked by long strips of colored cloth laid on the ground, and with colored smoke to guide our airmen during the mass bombing that preceded our breakout from the German ring that held us to the Normandy beachhead.

Dive-bombers hit it just right. We stood in the barnyard of a French farm and watched them barrel nearly straight down out of the sky. They were bombing about half a mile ahead of where we stood.

They came in groups, diving from every direction, perfectly timed, one right after another. Everywhere you looked separate groups of planes were on the way down, or on the way back up, or slanting over for a dive, or circling, circling, circling over our heads, waiting for their turn.

The air was full of sharp and distinct sounds of cracking bombs and the heavy rip of the planes' machine guns and the splitting screams of diving wings. It was all fast and furious, but yet distinct, as in a musical show in which you could distinguish throaty tunes and words.

And then a new sound gradually droned into our ears, a sound deep and all-encompassing with no notes in it – just a gigantic faraway surge of doom-like sound. It was the heavies. They came from directly behind us. At first they were the merest dots in the sky. You could see clots of them against the far heavens, too tiny to count individually. They came on with a terrible slowness.

Their march across the sky was slow and studied. I've never known a storm, or a machine, or any resolve of man that had about it the aura of such a ghastly relentlessness. You had the feeling that even had God appeared beseechingly before them in the sky with palms outward to persuade them back they would not have had within them the power to turn from their irresistible course.

The first huge flight passed directly over our farmyard and others followed. And then the bombs came. They began up ahead as the crackle of popcorn and almost instantly swelled into a monstrous fury of noise that seemed surely to destroy all the world ahead of us.

From then on for an hour and a half that had in it the agonies of centuries, the bombs came down. A wall of smoke and dust erected by them grew high in the sky. It filtered along the ground back through our own orchards. It sifted around us and into our noses. The bright day grew slowly dark from it.

By now everything was an indescribable cauldron of sounds. Individual noises did not exist. The thundering of the motors in the sky and the roar of bombs ahead filled all the space for noise on earth. Our own heavy artillery was crashing all around us, yet we could hardly hear it.

Further work on imagery

You have already seen that imagery can be very effective in making a description more powerful.

In **narrative** writing, it can help to engage and entertain the reader. In **non-narrative** writing, as you have already seen, it is often used to clarify, to illustrate and to convey the atmosphere of a scene or an event.

Read the following report, and then complete the tasks which follow.

Debris, Sunshine and Utter Silence

ON THE WESTERN FRONT, *August 21 1944* – When you're wandering around our very far-flung front lines – the lines that in our present rapid war are known as 'fluid' – you can always tell how recently the battle has swept on ahead of you.

You can sense it from the little things even more than the big things –

From the scattered green leaves and the fresh branches of trees still lying in the middle of the road.

From the wisps and coils of telephone wire, hanging brokenly from high poles and entwining across the roads.

From the gray, burned-powder rims of the shell craters in the gravel roads, their edges not yet smoothed by the pounding of military traffic.

From the little pools of blood on the roadside, blood that has only begun to congeal and turn black, and the punctured steel helmets lying nearby.

From the square blocks of building stone still scattered in the village street, and from the sharp-edged rocks in the roads, still uncrushed by traffic.

From the burned-out tanks and broken carts still unremoved from the road. From the cows in the fields, lying grotesquely with their feet to the sky, so newly dead they have not begun to bloat or smell.

From the scattered heaps of personal debris around a gun. (I don't know why it is, but the Germans always seem to take off their coats before they flee or die.)

From all these things you can tell that the battle has been recent – from these and from the men dead so recently that they seem to be merely asleep.

And also from the inhuman quiet. Usually battles are noisy for miles around. But in this recent fast warfare a battle sometimes leaves a complete vacuum behind it.

The Germans will stand and fight it out until they see there is no hope. Then some give up, and the rest pull and run for miles. Shooting stops. Our fighters move on after the enemy, and those who do not fight, but move in the wake of the battles, will not catch up for hours.

There is nothing left behind but the remains – the lifeless debris, the sunshine and the flowers, and utter silence.

An amateur who wanders in this vacuum at the rear of a battle has a terrible sense of loneliness. Everything is dead – the men, the machines, the animals – and you alone are left alive.

WS 6

TASK 9

In his report, Ernie Pyle says that you can tell how long ago the battle was fought because of 'the little things'. He then goes on to present a series of images of a village in the aftermath of battle.

Take each image listed below, and for each one, explain what aspect of war it brings to mind for you.

The first one is suggested for you.

'… scattered green leaves and the fresh branches of trees …'

'… telephone wire, hanging brokenly from high poles …'

'… the sharp-edged rocks in the roads …'

'… blood that has only begun to congeal and turn black …'

'… cows in the fields, lying grotesquely with their feet to the sky …'

'… the scattered heaps of personal debris around a gun …'

This is the debris of battle, but it also makes me think of how young, vigorous life has been ended by the war. The leaves were 'green', the branches 'fresh', and the soldiers very young.

TASK 10

Write a short account of Ernie Pyle's description, explaining what makes it an effective piece of writing.

In your account you should refer to:
- the *title*
- the *mood* of the piece of writing
- the *imagery*
- the author's use of *repetition*
- your feelings about the last sentence of the report
- any other aspect that you want to mention.

You should aim to write about 400–500 words.

Assessment – Everest

In this final section on descriptions, you are going to consider the types of passage and tasks that you are likely to encounter in your GCSE exam. You will be completing a response for reading and a response for writing.

Over the next two pages are two accounts of successful attempts to climb Mount Everest.

The first is by Stephen Venables, who reached the summit in 1988, and the second is by Jon Krakauer, who achieved the feat in disastrous circumstances in 1996, when eight climbers were lost.

Read the passages, and then complete the tasks which follow.

Stephen Venables

There were no clouds and the wind had dropped. We all thought we might pull it off. We climbed ten steps at a time, a slow plod. At 27,500 feet I felt incredibly sleepy. We were grinding to a halt. At one stage I sat down to have a snooze. Ed virtually caught up. I was hoping he would come and do some trail-breaking.

Apparently, I shouted: 'You're a bloody nuisance, I've been waiting here half an hour!' Then I took some caffeine pills and really improved; made a concentrated effort to move up the hill.

On the South Summit it was about 1.30pm. I realized that I could get to the summit by 4pm, and still get back again. Even when it got dark I'd be able to find my way with a head-torch. It was very hard to tell, but it seemed that I was making rational decisions and abiding by them. I was still in control. There comes a point when you have to stick your neck out a bit. After the South Summit there's some tricky climbing and I was pleased to find I could do it properly. I was still able to make moderately strenuous moves.

I thought the Hillary Step was a bit of an anti-climax. The snow on the right was quite firm. But it certainly is dramatic. There is this huge cornice, with 12,000 feet of East Face beneath. It's hard.

On the way down it got very hairy. The afternoon clouds came in. I felt awfully alone. My glasses were completely frozen over.

I was tired. Getting back to the South Summit I almost collapsed. I was hyper-ventilating; my glasses froze up; I had to take my mitten off to sort out the carabiner* to abseil over the Hillary Step. 'Jesus, this is hopeless,' I thought, 'I'll have to lie down and die.'

I really had to get a grip on myself. There were huge cornices over the East Face. I had to feel my way back.

*carabiner — a metal fastening, used to secure a rope

Jon Krakauer

Straddling the top of the world, one foot in China and the other in Nepal, I cleared the ice from my oxygen mask, hunched a shoulder against the wind, and stared absently down at the vastness of Tibet. I understood on some dim, detached level that the sweep of earth beneath my feet was a spectacular sight. I'd been fantasizing about this moment, and the release of emotion that would accompany it, for many months. But now that I was finally here, actually standing on the summit of Mount Everest, I just couldn't summon the energy to care.

It was early in the afternoon of May 10, 1996. I hadn't slept in fifty-seven hours. The only food I'd been able to force down over the preceding three days was a bowl of ramen soup and a handful of peanut M&Ms. Weeks of violent coughing had left me with two separated ribs that made ordinary breathing an excruciating trial. At 29,028 feet up in the troposphere, so little oxygen was reaching my brain that my mental capacity was that of a slow child. Under the circumstances, I was incapable of feeling much of anything except cold and tired.

Looking down the Southeast Ridge, the route we had ascended, training my lens on a pair of climbers approaching the summit, I noticed something that until that moment had escaped my attention. To the south, where the sky had been perfectly clear just an hour earlier, a blanket of clouds now hid Pumori, Ama Dablam, and the other lesser peaks surrounding Everest.

Nothing I saw early on the afternoon of May 10 suggested that a murderous storm was bearing down. To my oxygen-depleted mind, the clouds drifting up the grand valley of ice known as the Western Cwm looked innocuous, wispy, insubstantial. Gleaming in the brilliant midday sun, they appeared no different from the harmless puffs of convection condensation that rose from the valley almost every afternoon.

As I began my descent I was extremely anxious, but my concern had little to do with the weather: a check of the gauge on my oxygen tank had revealed that it was almost empty. I needed to get down, fast.

TASK 11– Reading

Compare the two accounts of the conquest of Everest. You should consider:
- the authors' descriptions of the scene
- their mental and physical condition
- their emotions.

You should aim to write about 250 words.

TASK 12– Writing

The climbing of Everest obviously offers the ultimate challenge to the mountaineer. However, all of us face challenges at one time or another – for example, examinations, tests, sporting finals, dance, music or drama productions. Write a 350–400 word article for your school magazine about a personal challenge that you faced.

REMEMBER

- you are **not** writing a story; rather, you are writing an **account**
- you should record **what happened** and **how you felt**
- you should try to convey the **atmosphere** of the event.

Printed below is a student's attempt at answering Task 12. It has been marked by a GCSE examiner. Read it through, and take note of the comments that the examiner has made.

A good opening which explains clearly the nature of the challenge.

It was on the 27th of June that I faced what I consider to be the greatest challenge of my life when I appeared in front of an audience of nearly four hundred people, playing the role of Sheila Birling in the school production of 'An Inspector Calls'.

Good use of language describing the rehearsals. The dreariness coupled with fear of the teacher's anger are both very nicely expressed. I particularly like the 'deathly cream colour' which captures the feelings of the actors very well.

Rehearsals had been difficult. They can often be dreary and painstakingly slow, but this year it seemed that there were more lengthy, pregnant pauses than ever, as actors dried up in the middle of speeches, turned a deathly cream colour, and waited for the tongue lashing that was sure to come from our director, Mrs Strickley.

It was difficult to decide how to play Sheila, for she is a character that seems to change over the course of the play. At the beginning she is petulant, rather silly, and seemingly very immature. However, she is an intelligent girl, and understands what the Inspector is doing far more clearly than any of the other characters.

Again, very good description in these two paragraphs. The two characters are very nicely drawn and the candidate certainly conveys the idea that all members of the cast were nervous but showed it in very different ways.

On the first night, all the actors were tense. Adrian Plummer, who played the Inspector, withdrew from the rest of the cast, sat on the floor of the dressing room with his back against the wall, and spent the next hour and a half silently mouthing his lines and beating his head against the brickwork whenever he made a mistake.

Jennifer Bayliss (Mrs Birling) was quite the opposite; she talked and joked with anybody who would listen to her, but the loudness of her voice betrayed the very thing that she was trying to disguise — like the rest of us, she was terrified.

Two really strong points here. Firstly, the candidate moves effortlessly from describing her own feelings to describing the scene in the auditorium. Secondly, it is so good to see a writer who can convey the tension of the situation by focusing on other things in addition to her sense of sight. The descriptions of the sounds and the heat are very good.

As for me, I kept asking myself why I was there. Why was I not 'out there' in the audience, ready to spend a relaxing, pleasant evening watching one of my favourite plays?

As the time ticked slowly round to 7.30, the auditorium began to fill up, and the isolated voices transformed into an expectant, excited hum, as the members of the audience claimed their seats, greeted their neighbours and began fanning their faces with their programmes as the temperature soared.

Nice contrast to the previous paragraph.

Silently, we all took our places at the table for the opening scene, all except for poor Adrian of course, who would have to suffer another quarter of an hour of agony before he could make his grand, forceful, impressive entrance on stage.

Good 'string' of adjectives here.

'Then' quickens the pace here, which reflects what is happening on the stage.

Then, almost before we knew what was happening, the house lights were snapped off, a couple of loud wolf whistles were hastily silenced and the curtains were swinging open to reveal the dark well of the auditorium.

My throat was suddenly parched, and my hands were trembling in my lap as my brain frantically rifled through its memory banks to try to remember the cue for my opening line.

Good use of paragraphing again, to change the focus. Also, some excellent descriptive detail (range of senses again) which conveys her fears very effectively.

Then Ben Harris, who played Gerald, gave me one of his warmest smiles, and suddenly, I was feeling fine. If he could do it, then so could I.

A very satisfying ending to the article — rounding the account off most successfully.

There we were, on stage, beautifully costumed, sitting in front of Mr Workman's magnificent set, performing for an audience of paying customers.

We would give them the performance of a lifetime!

Examiner's comments

This is a really excellent piece of work. It is accurate throughout, well structured and helpfully paragraphed.
   The candidate shows considerable expertise and has an excellent sense of audience; details are supplied appropriately, and she employs a wide vocabulary and a fluent style. Spelling and punctuation are faultless. I have no hesitation in awarding an A* for this work.

TASK 13

Here is the first side of another attempt to complete Task 12. Read it through, and then outline the **qualities** and **weaknesses** of the response. In doing this, you should refer to:

- content
- organisation
- paragraphing
- use of language
- punctuation and spelling.

The most chalenging thing I ever did was when we played in a cup finel at football, we played against parkfields School and we won two nil and I scored the second goal.

Before the game I was really nervus I had difficulty puting on my boots it was like my hands were cold. Mr Knight had told me that I would be playing in midfield, this is my favorite position so I thought things were going right and they were. When we got out onto the pitch my head nearly caved in when I saw how many people were their, nearly the whole school must of been out there and most of there school as well.

Their were lots of shouts from the tuchline, but I could hear one voice shouting out above all the others – my dad. As usual, he was telling me how I should play as if I didn't know. Anyway, we soon kicked off and we were lucky to survive in the first minute, their player went through on the goalkeeper but he pulled off a great save and got alot of applaws from all the people.

Then we went ahead, peter Curtis scored with a diving header and the crowd went mad (at least our lot did) Then it was really tiring cos the ground was soft and soon my legs started to feel like I had lead boots on. I looked at the crowd and realised that I couldn't let myself down I had to give everything I had got …

Unit 2 Information

Every day, we are bombarded with information.

Turn on the radio in the morning, and you will probably hear national news, local news, traffic news, sports reports and weather reports.

Get to school and the bombardment continues: information in assembly, information from form tutors, information from subject teachers. Then there are textbooks, worksheets, and a library full of encyclopaedias, newspapers and journals.

There are videos and CD-ROMs, and there's the Internet, an almost infinite bank of information, available to you at the touch of a few keys.

In this unit, you will be studying how to process and use this vast array of information, and how to write in an informative style.

In particular, you will be looking at:
- presenting your information
- selecting the right tone and register
- structuring an information text.

Presenting your information

Sometimes, information texts are laid out in simple prose style, and the layout of the text is relatively unimportant. Usually, however, information texts are laid out on the page very carefully, so that the information is presented clearly and key points are emphasised (look at this textbook, for example).

On this page and the next are some of the things you should look for when considering the layout of text.

Headings

Information texts need to gain the reader's attention quickly, and keep the reader interested in the information being given.

Large headings help to gain the attention of the reader. In some texts, like a school textbook, the heading may only tell you the subject of the text. In magazines or newspapers, on the other hand, headlines offer a sort of 'summary' of the article.

Subheadings

These are used to break up text and, like headings, draw the reader's attention to particular elements of the text. Scanning subheadings may help the reader to understand the shape of the piece of writing, or some of its main features. (How do subheadings help you to understand the teaching points on these two pages?)

Paragraphing

Many people are put off by large 'blocks' of print on a page. Therefore, information texts tend to contain relatively short paragraphs. Once more, you should notice how the paragraphing helps to draw attention to particular aspects of the writing. Consider, for example, whether different typefaces or 'fonts' have been used, or whether a particular paragraph is shaded, placed in a box, or set against a different coloured background. If any of those techniques have been used, what is their effect on the reader?

Diagrams, photographs and illustrations

You should take note of the **size** of the picture, and its **position** on the page.
- What is the picture drawing your attention to?
- How does it link with the text?

Captions

These are written under a picture, photograph, diagram, table and so on. They tell you what is in the picture etc., or comment on its content. Quite often, a caption gives a particular **interpretation** of an image. Notice how the captions below make you interpret the same image differently.

Stress in the workplace is becoming a serious problem in Britain today.

Businesswoman of the Year Kathy Campbell sealing another deal yesterday.

WS
8

TASK 1

Use the above information to help you to analyse the article on hang-gliders which is on the next two pages.

Analyse the layout of the text, by making a comment for each numbered section.

Remember, your comments should explain how the layout helps the reader to understand the article. For example:

1 The picture and caption help the reader to understand how hang-gliders are launched. It is also quite a dramatic, exciting picture, engaging the reader's attention.

29

1

2

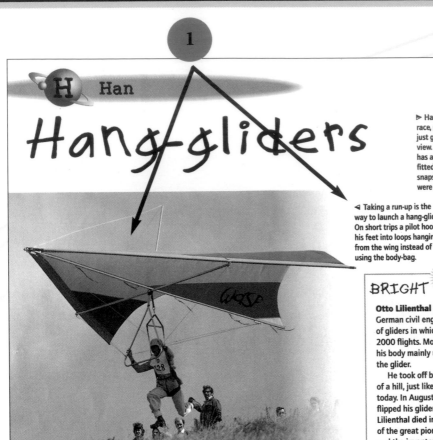

Hang-gliders

▷ Hang-glider pilots race, perform stunts or just go up to see the view. The body-bag has a camera pouch fitted so you can take snaps and prove you were up there!

◁ Taking a run-up is the way to launch a hang-glider. On short trips a pilot hooks his feet into loops hanging from the wing instead of using the body-bag.

BRIGHT SPARKS

Otto Lilienthal (1848-1896) was a German civil engineer who built a series of gliders in which he made more than 2000 flights. Most of his designs placed his body mainly underneath the wings of the glider.

He took off by running down the side of a hill, just like hang-gliders take off today. In August 1896, a gust of wind flipped his glider out of control and Lilienthal died in the crash. He was one of the great pioneers of manned flight and the inventor of the first successful hang-glider.

The closest man has come to flying through the air like a bird is by using a kite-like machine with no engine called a hang-glider. Hang-gliders are so called because the pilot hangs underneath the large, triangular wing of the glider.

A hang-glider's fuselage is the pilot suspended in a harness or body-bag. The harness is joined to the top of the triangular frame suspended beneath the wing. This is the A-frame.

PLASTIC NOSE

A hang-glider may have some basic flight instruments such as you find in an aircraft cockpit. These include a compass and an altimeter which tells the pilot how high up he or she is.

A moulded plastic nose cone on the point of the wing helps reduce drag from the air flowing over the hang-glider.

A hang-glider's wing can be 'tuned' to change the way it handles in the air. Tightening the sail improves its gliding performance. However, this makes the hang-glider harder to turn, so beginners often have the sail slackened to make it easier to handle.

The first harnesses hung underneath the hang-gliders were adapted from rock climbing harnesses. Now, they are specially designed, long fabric shells.

8

centre-line beam helps tilt and counter balance the wing

A-frame

harness

control bar

◁ **Reverse turn**
To turn left or right, the pilot pushes the control bar out to one side. Pushing the bar to the right, for example, causes the wing to dip down on the left, turning the hang-glider left.

◁ SEE ALSO ▷
Birds
Gliders
Microlights

10

9

3 **4**

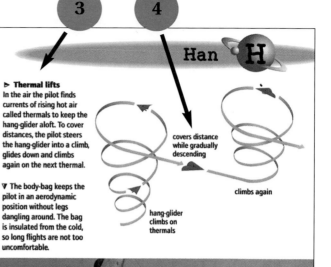

▷ **Thermal lifts**
In the air the pilot finds currents of rising hot air called thermals to keep the hang-glider aloft. To cover distances, the pilot steers the hang-glider into a climb, glides down and climbs again on the next thermal.

▽ The body-bag keeps the pilot in an aerodynamic position without legs dangling around. The bag is insulated from the cold, so long flights are not too uncomfortable.

covers distance while gradually descending

climbs again

hang-glider climbs on thermals

7

HANGING TOUGH

Unlike a glider or an ordinary aircraft, a hang-glider has no cockpit control surfaces. Instead, the pilot steers the craft by altering the position of his body weight. This, in turn, alters the position of the wing.

The pilot can push the control bar out from his body, tilting the wing back and causing the hang-glider to rise. Similarly, he can pull the bar towards him, which tips the wing down, making it descend. By routinely doing this, the pilot brings the hang-glider in to land.

TUDOR REALM

Experienced fliers soar on circles of hot air, called thermals, just like conventional gliders. These can keep a hang-glider airborne for two hours while it travels a distance of more than 150km. In 1978, a powered hang-glider crossed the English Channel for the first time; in 1990, an un-powered hang-glider, flown by Larry Tudor, managed a journey of 488km, a world record.

The Bare Bones

The glide angle is a measure of how well and for how long a hang-glider or conventional glider can travel forward as it descends towards the ground. The first hang-gliders had ratios of 1:2.5. This meant that they would drop 1m for every 2.5m they travelled forward. Modern hang-gliders now have glide angles of 1:14 or better.

6 **5**

Laying out your own page

The article below is adapted from *Which Way Now?*, a booklet published by the Department for Education and Employment. The booklet is written for Year 9 pupils, to help them in making decisions about which subjects they will take for GCSE.

Work in pairs to give the article more **impact** and to make it easier to read and **understand**. Use any of the following presentational devices:
- paragraphs (these could be boxed, shaded, etc.)
- bullet points
- numbers
- arrows
- subheadings
- diagrams/illustrations (with captions if necessary).

Where next?

Talk about hard work! You're still trying to decide what GCSE options to take, and you're already being asked what you're going to do after that. You don't have to make up your mind now about where you want to go after GCSEs, but two years go by fast, so it's worth checking out the possibilities now. You could stay on at school. If your school has a sixth form, you can study for A levels, AS levels, GNVQs or a mixture of these qualifications. You could go to college. You can study a wide range of courses, including A levels, AS levels and GNVQs, as well as vocational courses leading to City & Guilds diplomas, BTEC diplomas or NVQs. You can study part time at college, so you could be working at the same time. For many kinds of jobs now, you can get in by doing a Modern Apprenticeship or National Traineeship from the age of 16. You learn the skills you will need in your chosen career and get practical experience, and earn money at the same time. You'll also work towards recognised qualifications, usually NVQs. There are other ways to get training and qualifications, either while you are working, or from a specialist training company. You will often work towards NVQs as you gain skills in your chosen area of work. Another way of learning new skills and finding out about different types of work is as a volunteer. You could do anything from helping with environmental projects to working with elderly people or refugees. It can also be a way of learning about the community you live in. 'NVQ' stands for National Vocational Qualification. NVQ courses provide training for a specific job, and show that you have the real skills needed for that job.

Selecting the right tone and register

Audience

As with all texts, information texts vary enormously in the 'tone' or 'register' that they adopt. The way that they are written depends very much on the audience at whom they are aimed.

For instance, look at school textbooks. Textbooks written for an audience of younger children would certainly contain simpler language and sentence structure than, say, GCSE textbooks. You would also be likely to find more illustrations, and perhaps more humour.

Compare the ways in which the news is presented on *The Big Breakfast* and on *Sky News*; or compare the news reports on Radio 1 with the reports on Radio 4. The audiences for these programmes are very different, so the news reports are also very different, in the selection of material, the length of the news items, and the language used in the reports.

TASK 3

Printed below is an Internet page from 'Quit4life', which gives the Canadian public information on how to give up smoking, and the front page of a leaflet produced by the Health Education Authority.
- What is the **audience** for each leaflet?
- What **images** in the illustrations reflect this audience?

Now let us compare the information given in two articles. Look at the texts on the next two pages and then answer the questions which follow.

A

Tony's story - page 4

Back Forward Stop Refresh Home Favorites History Search AutoFill Larger Smaller Print Mail Preferences

Address: http://www.quit4life.com/html/tony/tony4.html Go

Live Home Page | Apple Computer | Apple Support | Apple Store | MSN | Office for Macintosh

Favorites | History | Search | Page Holder

QUIT4LIFE

Concern about gaining weight is a roadblock for some smokers. While you may gain some weight after quitting, it can be controlled by what you eat and by regular physical activity. Here are some tips to help:

- Eat breakfast! This kickstarts your body's metabolism.
- Drink plenty of water (6–8 glasses a day)
- Eat low-fat, low-calorie foods
- Eat more fruit, vegetables and whole grains
- Avoid coffee and sweets
- Chew sugarless gum
- Chew on a toothpick, munch on raw vegetables, drink ice water, play cards, doodle, do a crossword puzzle or jigsaw puzzle – clean up your bedroom, try acuuming, play an instrument, listen to music, watch television, or anything else that will distract you from smoking.
- Reward yourself for not smoking – go to a movie, have a manicure, buy yourself a pair of jeans or a new CD with the money you save by not smoking.
- Set up smoke-free zones – clean up any places where you used to smoke, such as your car, bedroom or recreation room, and make them off-limits to smoking by anyone.

Aw, man, it's not worth it. I gotta be in there.

First, I'm gettin' rid of these things for good.

Spin 4 Life

back Crunch time, Clock running down. What's the call, Tony?

Internet zone

B

HOW TO KICK THE HABIT

Pregnancy is one of the best chances you will ever have to give up smoking. Almost half those women who stop while pregnant, stay stopped. So don't waste this opportunity.

It is never too late. Your baby's health chances improve the day you stop. If you fail, try again. Each week without cigarettes is a better week for your baby.

Follow this stop smoking plan

1. Set a date to stop
Choose a day when you are likely to be relaxed. Get rid of all your cigarettes, ashtrays and lighters the night before.

2. Think about why you smoke
Here are some possibilities: 'It helps me relax', 'It stops me feeling hungry', 'I'm afraid I'll put on weight'.

Knowing why you smoke will help you to find the reasons to stop.

● Cigarettes don't calm your nerves, they just calm the craving for nicotine, which they also create.
● If cigarettes dampen your appetite then that is a good reason to stop. You need to eat well during pregnancy. By the time the baby is born you will be a non-smoker.

3. Break the links which create the habit
● If tea or coffee and cigarettes always go together, perhaps you should try drinking something different.
● Avoid smoky places: ask friends to meet you at home.
● If your hands feel empty, try knitting, or doing your nails.
● If watching TV makes you want to smoke, put on your coat and take a walk around the block.

In time the urge will fade and you can happily return to your old routines.

4. Get support
Tell everyone around you what you're doing and why. Ask them not to offer you cigarettes. Your partner can help best by giving up too or at least not smoking near you.

5. Take one day at a time
Forever seems like a very long time, so don't think about it. Just stick with being a non-smoker *today*.

6. Learn to relax
Relaxation techniques are often taught in ante-natal classes, or you could borrow a relaxation tape from the library. The technique will be a great help when the baby comes.

7. Expect to feel rough
Nicotine in cigarettes is addictive. If you were a heavy smoker your body will have to get used to managing without. You may be lucky and notice little change, but you may also feel irritated and light-headed, find it hard to concentrate and even hard to sleep. Many women feel these things when they are pregnant anyway, so that makes pregnancy an even better time to stop smoking. The feelings are only temporary.

8. Reward yourself
Save your cigarette money and use it to buy yourself a little gift at the end of the first week. You've earned it! You might choose to save up the money, perhaps using a chart on the wall to remind you. In a year's time you'll have saved for a well-earned family holiday!

TASK 4

a) What is the **focus** of the introductory paragraph of the Quit4life article A?

b) What is the **focus** of the introduction to the Health Education Authority article B?

c) Compare the **content** of the two articles. How does the advice differ? In answering, refer closely to the texts to support your viewpoint.

d) Can you give any instances of how the **language** used in the two articles reflects the audiences for whom the articles were intended? Again, be specific, and refer closely to the text to support your answer.

The nature of the information

This will make a difference to how the text is written. For instance, a report of a dog running around Wimbledon's Centre Court and halting a match would probably demand a humorous approach, whereas a report of, say, a train crash would always be treated with seriousness and gravity.

Formal or informal language?

The **audience** for whom the information is written, and the **nature** of the information, will largely determine the type of language used in an information text.

Formal language follows recognisable rules of grammar and punctuation, and the tone is serious, impersonal and businesslike. Points are made clearly and concisely. For instance, if you were giving information about yourself in a letter of application for a job, you would probably adopt a 'formal' tone:

> *I was appointed as a school prefect in September, and my duties are to supervise children over the lunch hour and ...*

Informal language is friendly and conversational. If you wrote a letter to a friend or relative, then you would use an 'informal' tone:

> *You'll never guess! I've been made a prefect, and do you know what I'm expected to do? You won't believe me, but I'm supposed to keep the kids quiet in the lunch queue! Me – Motormouth!*

WS 9

TASK 5

With a partner, discuss and write down five information texts in which you would expect the language used to be *formal*, five in which you would expect to see *informal* language and three in which the language would be likely to be a mixture of the two. Use a table like the one below. An example of each has been done for you.

Formal	Informal	Mixture of both
Letter of application for a job	Letter to a friend or relation	Article in a teenage football magazine

On this page and the next are three accounts of Sparta, a state in Ancient Greece. Read the texts carefully and then answer the questions which follow. These will help you to compare the **tone** or **register** of the three pieces of writing.

The state determined whether children, both male and female, were strong when they were born; weakling infants were left in the hills to die of exposure. Exposing weak or sickly children was a common practice in the Greek world, but Sparta institutionalized it as a state activity rather than a domestic activity. At the age of seven, every male Spartan was sent to military and athletic school. These schools taught toughness, discipline, endurance of pain (often severe pain), and survival skills. At twenty, after thirteen years of training, the Spartan became a soldier. The Spartan soldier spent his life with his fellow soldiers; he lived in barracks and ate all his meals with his fellow soldiers. He also married, but he didn't live with his wife; one Athenian once joked that Spartans had children before they even saw the faces of their wives. The marriage ceremony had an unusual ritual involved: at the end of the ceremony, the man carried his wife off as if he were taking her by force.

Ancient Greece: Sparta
by Richard Law

Sparta had no tyrants. Her effective government appears to have been shared between a council of old men and five magistrates called 'ephors', while the two hereditary kings had special military powers. These oligarchs* were in the last resort answerable to the assembly of the Spartiates (of whom, according to Herodotus, there were early in the fifth century about five thousand). Sparta was, therefore, a large aristocracy whose origin, ancient writers agreed, was the hoplite* class. Society remained agricultural; no commercial class was allowed to appear and when the rest of Greece took up the use of money, around 600 BC, Sparta stood out and permitted only an iron currency for internal use. Spartiates were not supposed to own silver or gold until the fourth century.

This produced a sort of militarized egalitarianism* often admired by later puritans*, and an atmosphere strongly suggestive, for good and ill, of the aspirations of the more old-fashioned English public school. Though the passing of time and the position of kings slightly softened their practice, Spartiates knew no great distinctions of wealth or comfort. Until well into classical times they avoided dressing differently and ate at communal messes. Their conditions of life were, in a word, 'spartan', reflecting the idealization of military values and strict discipline. The details are often strikingly unpleasant as well as curious. Marriage, for example, was a ceremony for which the bride's hair was cropped and she was dressed as a boy. It was followed by a simulated rape, after which the couple did not live together, the man continuing to live with his companions in the male dormitory and eating in messes with them.

History of the World by J. M. Roberts

oligarchs – members of a small ruling class

hoplite – heavily armed foot soldier

egalitarianism – asserting the equality of mankind

puritans – people with extremely strict moral or religious views

THE SAVAGE SPARTANS

The first great state to grow after the Dark Ages was Sparta. The Spartan people were a bit odd. They believed they were better than anyone else. If the Spartans wanted more land then they just moved into someone else's patch. If someone else was already living there the Spartans just made them slaves. In short, they were the ungrooviest lot in the whole of Greece.

Of course, a lot of people didn't enjoy being slaves. They argued with the Spartans in the only language the Spartans knew – the language of violence. They were probably the toughest of the Greek peoples, because they were always having to fight to prove how good they were.

But it wasn't enough to train young men to fight. The training started from the day you were born.

SOME FOUL FACTS

1 Children were trained for fitness with running, wrestling, throwing quoits and javelins – and that was just the girls!

2 The marriage custom of Sparta was for a young man to pretend to carry his bride off by violence. The bride then cut off her hair and dressed like a man. The bridegroom rejoined the army and had to sneak off to visit his new wife.

3 A new-born baby was taken to be examined by the oldest Spartans. If it looked fit and strong they said, 'Let it live.' If it looked a bit sickly it was taken up a mountain and left to die.

4 A child didn't belong to its parents – it belonged to the State of Sparta. At the age of seven a child was sent off to join a 'herd' of children. The toughest child was allowed to become leader and order the others about. The old men who watched over them often set the children fighting amongst each other to see who was the toughest.

5 At the age of 12 they were allowed a cloak but no tunic. They were only allowed a bath a few times a year.

6 Children slept on rushes that they gathered from the river bank themselves. If they were cold in winter then they mixed a few thistles in with the reeds … the prickling gave them a feeling of warmth.

Horrible Histories – The Groovy Greeks by Terry Deary, illustrated by Martin Brown

WS
10

TASK 6

a) Look first at the *content* of the three passages – the things that the authors have chosen to write about.
  - What similarities can you find in terms of content?
  - What differences can you find?

b) Now take each passage in turn. How would you describe the *tone* of each passage?
  - Is it serious?
  - Is there humour in the article?
  - Is it sarcastic?
  - Is the language used formal and impersonal, or lighthearted and conversational?

Explain your answers fully – the tone of the passage may not always fit into a single 'category', but may be a mixture of more than one. Remember to support all your observations with evidence by quoting briefly from the passage.

c) Who do you think the *audience* would be for each piece of writing? Explain why you came to this conclusion.

TASK 7

Imagine that you are an historian, looking back on life in Britain in the late twentieth and early twenty-first centuries. Write two accounts, giving information about society in Britain. You might write about the sorts of lives people led, and the main features of the age. (What do you think would be the 'main features' of the age? Wars? The motor car? Television and cinema? Computers? The Internet?)

One account should be written in the tone of *History of the World*, and the other in the tone of *Horrible Histories*. Write about 200 words for each.

Structuring information texts

Narrative texts – stories – often follow a very simple 'What happened next?' structure. So, a plan for a story about a day trip to a theme park might be:

- waking up and the excitement of preparing for the day
- meeting the coach and a description of the trip to the park
- describing the 'Black Hole', 'Tunnel of Fear' and 'Space Walk' rides
- exhaustion at the end of the day – sleeping on the coach
- arrival back at school.

You can see how this plan follows a 'What happened next?' structure.

What makes informative writing more difficult is that usually it does not follow such a structure.

For instance, if you were writing an article about a new car, you would need to think about the 'topic areas' that you might want to write about. Below is a possible plan, which includes information about a new car, the RX-7.

You could plan your article like this:

Safety:
ABS braking system, two airbags, collapsible steering column.

Performance:
Top speed 130 mph. Acceleration 0–60 in 4.1 seconds. 24 mpg.

Interior:
Leather seats, deep - pile carpets, polished walnut dashboard.

The RX-7

Comfort:
Lack of leg room, air - conditioning, very little engine noise.

Design features:
Long bonnet, alloy wheels, tinted glass, concealed headlights.

Sound system:
CD, radio and cassette player: six speakers – four front and two rear.

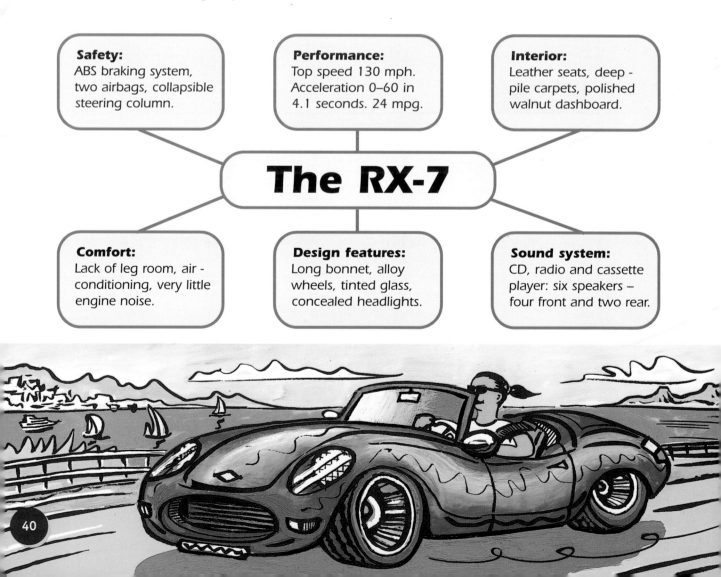

This plan gives you six topic paragraphs, and you need to decide in which order to present them.

There seems to be a natural division here that is helpful in working out an order: three sections give specifications for the car, and three sections deal with the interior. Therefore, it might be sensible to present the information in this order:

- performance
- safety
- design features
- interior
- comfort
- sound system.

This is not the only order possible, however. You might think of another order which is equally logical. The important thing is that there is a *pattern* or *logic* in the structure of the writing.

You will also need an **introductory paragraph**, perhaps referring to the car's country of origin, its launch date, price, etc.

At the end of your article, you will need a **concluding paragraph**, perhaps giving an overall view of the car, or considering the cars that will oppose it in the market.

TASK 8

Write an article of about 250–300 words for *Motoring Magazine*, in which you give readers information about the launch of the RX-7. You should expand on the information given on the opposite page, and remember to paragraph your work to help the reader. The article has been started below.

RX-7 launched next month

All the hype surrounding the development of the RX-7 comes to a climax next month with its launch at this year's Motor Show.
— Introduction

It certainly is a very classy performer, if the official figures are anything to go by. It boasts a top speed of 130 miles per hour, and accelerates from 0–60 in a hair-raising 4.1 seconds. Yet surprisingly, the car is also reasonably economical for a car of its type, managing an average 24 miles on a gallon of fuel.
— First topic paragraph: main idea followed by supporting details.

TASK 9

The passage below is taken from *Which?*, a consumer magazine which reviews various products from board games to holidays. In this case, large family cars have been tested, and the article below outlines some of the strengths and weaknesses of the Toyota Avensis.

The article was written in six paragraphs. Decide what these paragraphs should be, and write out the first two or three words of each paragraph, followed by the last two or three.

Then, summarise the main idea of each paragraph in a few words of your own.

Finally, list the details which support the main idea. The first one has been done for you.

<u>Para 1</u> The Avensis ... the steering precise.

<u>Main idea</u>
This paragraph tells the reader about how well the car handles.

<u>Supporting details</u>
Responsive engine, smooth gear change, heavy/easy-to-use clutch, smooth brakes, confident handling, precise steering.

The Avensis was the favourite of this group with our panel of drivers. They praised the car's responsive engine, which accelerated well across the rev range. The gear change was smooth, but opinion was divided over the clutch: some of our drivers found it easy to use, but others found it heavy. The brakes, too, were smooth and progressive. The car's handling was confident, and the steering precise. The front and rear seats offered good support and reasonable legroom, though headroom was limited for taller passengers, especially in the rear. Most major controls, including the pedals and steering wheel, were well placed, although some drivers criticised the position of the handbrake, which they felt was too close to their knee. Luggage space in the Avensis was adequate, but intrusive large wheel arches and a narrow hatch opening made the space less useful than it could be. The high rear shelf obstructed the view out of the back, but large door mirrors gave a clear rearward view. Ride comfort was a particular strongpoint: the car remained composed over all types of road surface. Noise was minimal – in fact, some people found the lack of engine noise disconcerting. The car's heating and ventilation system was effective and easy to use. The Avensis was the best car of this group for security, though there's still room for improvement. On the plus side, it had an alarm as standard and a non-standard shape stereo system, which should make it less attractive to thieves. The car's doors resisted our 'thief's' attempts for well over a minute, though they did not have deadlocks. The 'open' design of the Avensis' front head restraints, and the internal structure of the rear ones, may not provide the best protection in rear-impact accidents. The steering column and other components posed a threat to the driver's knees in a crash. The car had side airbags and meets forthcoming legislation on side-impact protection. A three-point seat belt was provided in the centre rear seat. In general, the rear seat belts could be a little inconvenient to use after the seat was folded forward. There was good advice on child restraints in the car's handbook.

Which? online February 1999

Assessment – the sinking of the *Titanic*

The luxury liner *Titanic* sank on its maiden voyage in April 1912, and on 26 June 1913 the district court of the Southern District of New York published a digest of witnesses' statements. The testimonies on this page and the next have been dramatised from that digest.

Read through the extracts, and then complete the task which follows.

Testimony of Joseph Bruce Ismay

Question: You are the Chief Executive Officer of the Oceanic Steam Navigation Company, owner of the *Titanic*?
Answer: That is correct, Sir.
Question: Tell me, Mr Ismay, were you aware that the *Titanic* was not equipped with lifeboats to carry anywhere near the amount of passengers on board?
Answer: I was aware of that, Sir.
Question: Did you do anything about it, or suggest to others that they might do something?
Answer: No, Sir.
Question: Why not?
Answer: We believed the ship to be absolutely unsinkable, Sir.
Question: Did you know about the presence of ice in the area?
Answer: Yes, Sir, we had received a Marconigram to that effect, and I advised Captain Smith to increase the speed of the vessel to help to break up any ice ...

Testimony of G. Symons

Question: At what speed were you travelling?
Answer: About 22½ knots, Sir.
Question: Did you have good vision ahead of you on the night in question?
Answer: Not really, Sir. You see, there was some haze before the accident. Also, no binoculars were furnished to the lookouts, so they could not detect ice ahead. And, in truth, the sea was very flat that night, so there would have been no spray on the edge of the ice.
Question: But none the less, you were informed of an iceberg up ahead?
Answer: Yes, Sir. A message to that effect did reach the bridge.
Question: Did the vessel slow down as it reached the danger zone?
Answer: It did not, Sir. Neither did it attempt to change course and so avoid the ice.
Question: I understand that in weather conditions like you describe, it is usual to double the lookouts. Did this happen on 14th April?
Answer: No, Sir, it did not.
Question: One final question, Mr Symons. Were any lifeboat drills held during the voyage?
Answer: No, Sir. Please remember that we had only been sailing for a few days ...

Testimony of Edward Wilding

Question: Mr Wilding, you are an eminent ship designer. I believe that despite the claim that the *Titanic* was unsinkable, you yourself had doubts.

Answer: I wouldn't say that I had doubts about the ship at the time. I believe I shared everyone's confidence in it. However, the vessel did not have an inner skin. Had it done so, it would probably not have sunk. Similarly, it had no watertight decks, except for the weather deck. I believe that if watertight bulkheads had been carried up to C deck, the ship would probably have been able to stay afloat.

Question: That is indeed an interesting observation, Mr Wilding. Now, let us turn our attention to the lifeboats. Most of them were lowered less than half full.

Answer: Yes, they were, and I don't see any practical reason for that. The lifeboats were strong enough to carry 65 people, having been constructed to be so used and tested to that extent; that should have been a matter of general knowledge. The lifeboat falls were tested to hold about 50 tons, and a full lifeboat would weigh only about $5\frac{1}{2}$ tons ...

Testimony of Sir Ernest Shackleton

Question: Sir Ernest, you have much experience of ice from your exploration of the Antarctic. Could you tell the court if icebergs can be easily spotted?

Answer: No, they cannot. Some bergs appear black and do not reflect the light in any way.

Question: So they are invisible?

Answer: Not exactly, but they are generally seen better from down near the water-line. In a dead calm sea, there is no sign to indicate a berg's existence, so I would always post a look-out as close to the water-line as possible, as well as one in the crow's nest, if ice was in the area.

Question: I see. Would the captain have known of the presence of ice, in your opinion, Sir Ernest?

Answer: Yes, he would.

Question: Why so?

Answer: Ice in the Atlantic drifts south from the north, with the Labrador current. Also, I am given to understand that on the night in question there was no wind, and there had been an abnormal fall of temperature. This should have provided a very clear indication of the presence of ice.

TASK 10

a) List all the factors you believe contributed to the sinking of the *Titanic*, then list the factors that led to so many people perishing, rather than being saved.

b) Now write a report of about 350 words to the Oceanic Steam Navigation Company, giving information about the faults in the design of the *Titanic*, and commenting on the actions of her crew.

REMEMBER

- **organise** your lists so you can present your views in logical order
- **paragraph** your writing to reflect such organisation
- consider other **presentational devices**, such as bullet points or subheadings
- use **language** that is appropriate to the **task** and the **audience**
- use the **main idea/supporting details** structure to help you to shape your writing.

Printed below is a student's attempt at answering Task 9. It has been marked by a GCSE examiner. Read it through, and take note of the comments that the examiner has made.

Apostrophes used incorrectly throughout, indicating where the two words have been telescoped together, rather than showing where a letter has been missed out.

A number of points made in the text have been correctly selected here, but the paragraph is totally disorganised.

> I have been thinking about all the evidence that has been put forward and I think the Oceanic Steam Navigation Company is at fault because the captain did'nt know what he was doing and the ship was'nt good enough.
>
> The ship did'nt have enough lifeboats so that when it sank most people could'nt be saved. This is very bad. Also there was only one lookout and there should have been two. If the ship had got an inner skin, it might not have sunk. The captain had received a radio message so why did'nt he know about the ice, I mean he was the captain after all so he should know about these things.
>
> Finally there had been no lifeboat drills so that is why so many people died and why the company is at fault.

An attempt at an introductory paragraph which does, at least, indicate two 'main ideas'.
However, the tone of the writing is too informal. For instance, I would expect something like: 'I believe that the captain made some inappropriate decisions that led directly to the sinking of the vessel.'

Not really a concluding paragraph. Another detail is introduced, and this should have been included earlier.

<u>Examiner's comments</u>

The task was set in two distinct parts: the factors that contributed to the <u>sinking</u> of the 'Titanic', and secondly, the factors which led to so many people dying. While the candidate has given some details about both of these elements he has made no attempt to organise them, and this is a serious weakness of the response. For example, the first detail given refers to the lifeboats, but the candidate then skips on through other details, before returning to the subject of the lifeboats. Candidates should understand that responses must be <u>structured</u> logically, and that clear paragraphing can help to demonstrate this structure.

However, it is also clear that a number of points have been omitted, which is unsurprising, as the candidate only wrote to about one third of the required length. Word limits are suggested advisedly: if the examiners suggest a limit of 350 words, they do so because they believe that the task will require a response of this length in order to cover all the points that need to be made.

In addition, the candidate's use of language was not appropriate either to the task or the audience.

In conclusion, the response may gain a <u>very low</u> GCSE grade, as the candidate did demonstrate some understanding of the passage, and did manage to draw out a few relevant points, but it could certainly expect no higher reward than that.

TASK 11

Here is the first side of another attempt at answering Task 10.

Read it through, and then outline the **qualities** and **weaknesses** of the response. In doing this, you should refer to:

- content
- organisation
- paragraphing and other presentational devices
- use of language
- spelling
- understanding of main idea/supporting details structure.

Having considered all the evidence provided by the testimony of the witnesses, I have come to the conclusion that the 'Titanic' had serious design faults which caused the problem.

Firstly, Mr Whiting, a ship designer, told the court how the 'Titanic' did not have an inner skin and that if it had it properly wouldn't have sunk. Also, it didn't have enough lifeboats for all the passengers.

The captain of the ship must take a lot of stick as well for what he did, or rather what he didn't do.

He should of known about the ice in the area because he was warned about this on the radio. Also there was no wind and it was very cold. He didn't do anything, though. In fact, he actually speeded up because he thought that it would help to break up the ice, which is ridiculous. However, he did this on the advice of Joseph Ismay, who was the Chief Executive Officer, so it wasn't all the captain's fault.

The weather was also very bad that night and there was a haze, but the really amazing thing is that the lookouts still didn't have any binoculars. Now I would of thought that lookouts should always have binoculars, especially in poor weather, and especially when they know that there is ice in the area. Again, I blame the captain for this.

Unit 3 Explanation

An explanation is an account which tries to communicate meaning – usually by answering the questions 'how?' or 'why?'. For example, you could explain how a car engine works, or why you are an hour late for an appointment!

Explanations can appear in many forms: letters, manuals, leaflets, personal accounts, newspaper/magazine articles and emails are just some examples.

When writing explanations, as with all texts, you must ensure that you understand why you are writing the explanation – your **purpose** – and who it is aimed at – your **audience**.

Although important in all types of writing, the audience is particularly important when writing explanations. As well as fairly common factors such as the age and the gender of your intended audience, you will need to take into account such things as how much knowledge and experience of the subject matter they will have.

In this unit, you will be studying how the purpose and audience alter the type of language used, the amount of detail you include and the form of the explanation.

Audience

Below and on the next page are three extracts from books which explain what a transistor is and how it works.

A 1 A small positive electrical charge is sent down one aluminium lead that runs into the transistor. The positive charge is transferred to a layer of conductive polysilicon buried in the middle of nonconductive silicon dioxide.

2 The positive charge attracts negatively charged electrons out of the base of P-type (positive) silicon that separates two layers of N-type (negative) silicon.

3 The rush of electrons out of the P-type silicon creates an electronic vacuum that is filled by electrons rushing from another conductive lead called the *source*. In addition to filling the vacuum in the P-type silicon, the electrons from the source also flow to a similar conductive lead called the *drain*, completing the circuit and turning the transistor on so that it represents a 1 bit. If a negative charge is applied to the polysilicon, electrons from the source are repelled and the transistor is turned off.

B Transistors are small ELECTRONIC devices. They are usually made to amplify (strengthen) electric currents in electronic equipment such as radios, televisions, computers and satellites. They can also switch electric currents on and off. Transistors have largely replaced other devices, called valves, which were once used for the same purpose.

Today complicated circuits containing thousands of transistors can be put into SILICON CHIPS that are only a centimetre square. The first practical transistors were developed in the 1940s by the American scientists Walter Brattain, John Bardeen and William Shockley. The invention of transistors completely revolutionized electronics and millions of these devices are now made every year.

A transistor in a circuit (left), and shown in section (right). The transistor shown here is made of a sandwich of three differently treated pieces of silicon. This type of transistor amplifies a signal and has the same effect as the more old-fashioned triode valve. The flow of electrons is shown by the blue arrows.

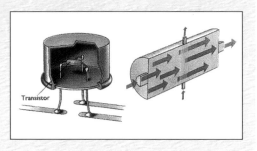

C How a transistor works

A transistor contains a sandwich of three pieces of a semiconductor, usually silicon. The outer pieces (the collecter and emitter) are connected to a strong power supply. The central piece (the base) resists the flow of current through the transistor. When a weak electric signal is input to the base, however, the resistance of the base is lowered, allowing the strong current to flow into the collector, through the base, and out of the emitter.

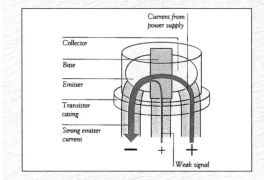

Variations in the level of the weak signal are transferred to the strong current, which emerges as an amplified copy of the weak signal.

Controlling power
Amplifiers use a small force to control a large force. Aerosol sprays do this: a weak force from a finger controls the high-pressure spray.

Amplifying a weak signal
A weak signal allows a strong current to pass.

WS
15

TASK 1

For each text, work out the intended audience. Look at the clues provided and try to be as specific as possible, including such information as likely age.
Explain how you came to your decision for each text by referring to:
- the level of language
- sentence length
- how much (if any) prior knowledge is assumed (think about the use of jargon and/or technical expressions)
- tone
- style.

TASK 2

Here are the front covers of the books from which each extract was taken.

Match each text with its cover, and explain why you made each choice.

Tone

Tone can play a large part in gaining the interest of an audience and therefore making an explanation more effective. Traditionally, explanations in textbooks tended to be written in a very formal style and the tone was serious. Many school books adopted this approach, with the result that they sometimes did not appeal to the pupils who were reading them. Today, much more emphasis is placed on making texts more interesting and varied.

Look at the example below and on the opposite page. It explains the functions of various parts of the human digestive system.

The life-saving liver
Tiny bits of digested food molecules in the blood go to the liver to make vital substances your body needs. The liver also does hundreds of other vital jobs such as making bile.

The vagus (vay-gus) nerve
The vagus nerve is like a long telephone wire that 'vaguely' snakes round the guts carrying messages to and from the brain. These include orders to squeeze the gut wall and move the food ball on to its next destination.

TASK 3

a) In what ways do the explanations on these two pages differ from a 'traditional' textbook? Think about the layout, illustrations, vocabulary and humour.

b) Who do you think is the intended audience? Why do you think this?

c) Re-write the information using Standard English and no illustrations.

d) What difference do the changes which you have made make to the tone of the text? Are the explanations as clear? What effect do you think the changes would have on the original audience?

Crucial kidneys

These are the body's filters. As blood passes through them they clear out all the spare water and waste products and send them down for storage in the bladder.

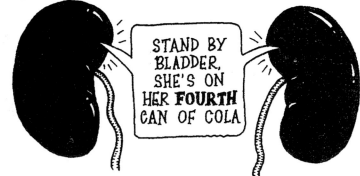

Bursting bladder

This is an incredibly wrinkled sack. It looks like a prune after a really long bath, but as it fills up, it gets bigger and it looks more like a balloon. The speed this happens depends on how much a person has had to drink. Most people need to pee about four to six times a day.

How can you tell when someone's bladder is full? Easy. They start twitching, writhing and dancing around looking for the nearest loo. If you were feeling heartless you could…

Horrible Science - Disgusting Digestion by Nick Arnold, illustrated by Tony de Saulles

Features of explanations

Explanations generally have to answer the question 'why?' or 'how?'. Before you begin to write an explanation, especially if it is in an examination, you need to think about and plan your writing very carefully. You will need to ensure that your explanation is:

Clear

- the text needs to be understood easily and you must be careful, for example, not to repeat information
- if you need to use technical terms or jargon, you should be sure that your audience will know what is meant; if you are not sure that they will do so, you will need to define these terms when you first mention them, or provide a glossary which can be easily accessed
- presentational devices such as subheadings, subtitles or illustrations can help to make the finished text look clearer, less cluttered and more appealing.

Concise

- you will need to write in complete sentences, often using quite complex terminology. Avoid over-long sentences, which can become difficult to follow
- remember that too much information may confuse your audience.

Logical

- one of the main features of a successful explanation is that each piece of information is carefully organised into a logical sequence.

TASK 4

Study the leaflet on the next page carefully.

a) How far does it fulfil each of the above criteria for a successful explanatory text?

b) What would you change in order to make the explanation clearer and easier to follow?

c) Some parts of this text are not strictly explanations. Try to identify these. Why do you think they have been included in the leaflet?

Ebenezer Sneezer's

Guide to Colds and Flu

We all get colds and flu.
On average, we get at least two colds a year

They always seem to come at the worst possible time. For example, when you're:

busy at work

busy with the kids

getting ready for the social event of the year

There's no need to suffer and miss out...

Cold and flu symptoms are very similar, but there are some important differences. You can use this leaflet to help you decide which illness you have, what treatments you could use, whether or not you need to see your doctor and what you can do to make yourself feel better.

Colds and flu are caused by viruses. Antibiotics do not kill viruses and, despite years of research, there is still no medicine which will cure your cold or flu. What you can do is relieve the symptoms, such as runny nose, sore throat, headache and fever. Taking vitamin C and zinc supplements can help defend your body against infection. Most of the symptoms you get from a cold or flu are the result of your body fighting the virus. **Stopping the symptoms does not get rid of the virus.**

What happens when you get a cold or flu?

The viruses which cause colds and flu are spread in tiny droplets produced when an infected person breathes, coughs or sneezes. They get into your body through your eyes or as you breathe. When the cells that protect your nose and throat from infection fail to stop the virus, you get a cold or flu. The virus uses the cells in your nose and throat to reproduce itself. You will get a sore throat, runny nose and start sneezing as your body begins to get rid of the infected cells. **Sneezing is an early warning - so this is the time to start treating the symptoms.**

Within 24 hours the infected cells have released chemicals to attract white blood cells to fight the virus. This causes inflammation in your nose and throat, giving you that blocked-up stuffy feeling. Your body may also release histamine, a substance which encourages your body to release mucus. This gives you a runny nose, a cough and it may also make you sneeze. **If you have flu,** you will be feverish and the virus will produce toxins which will make your muscles ache.

After four or five days, if your body's first response to the infection has not killed off the cold virus, your temperature may rise as two more types of white blood cell join the attack. This does not mean that the cold has turned into flu. You will feel more tired and sluggish because your body is using more energy to fight the virus and because it has lasted for a few days. You will also find your nose is more blocked-up, or that you perhaps have pain around your eyes caused by blocked sinuses. You may still have a cough even after your cold has disappeared.

Coughs and sneezes spread diseases. An average sneeze will spread over 100,000 virus cells up to 30 feet (9 metres)... ...that's the length of a big red London bus.

The fastest sneeze recorded was 103.6mph... ...that's four times faster than Linford Christie.

When you sneeze your heart stops beating, you stop breathing and you close your eyes... ...if you are driving when you sneeze, you are blind for up to 300 feet (91 metres).

Using illustrations

Illustrations are often used to help explain how something works. Photographs, diagrams and cartoons, for example, can all be used to make an explanation clearer to the intended audience.

Look at the example below, which shows how a vacuum flask works.

How a vacuum flask is made
The vacuum flask is the best kind of thermal flask. It can keep liquids hot or cold for many hours. It is basically a 'double-skinned' glass bottle.

A space without air or any other substance is called a **vacuum.** In a vacuum there is nothing to pass on the heat, so no heat can be lost or gained. The inner bottle of a vacuum flask is sealed to the outer one and nearly all the air is pumped out to make a vacuum

Glass is a strong material even when it is thin. It is easy to coat with silver and it does not take up or give out flavours to the liquids it contains

Silvering bounces back, or reflects, heat waves. The inside silvering on the vacuum flask reflects most of the heat back into the flask, keeping the liquid hot.
   The outer silvering bounces away any heat trying to get in to the flask. This is important when trying to stop a cold liquid from heating up

Plastic case to cushion against shocks

TASK 5

Choose an everyday item from around the home or school. Using diagrams and captions where necessary, explain how it works.

Now look carefully at the illustration below. It is by William Heath Robinson.
He used illustrations in a humorous way to demonstrate ingenious labour-saving devices.

*A new machine for
picking up matches
and cigarette-ends.*

TASK 6

Write two explanations of how the machine in the illustration works. In both cases
your audience is pupils of your own age.

Your first explanation should be written to accompany the illustration. You could, if
you wish, use arrows to show which part of the machine you are explaining.

Your second explanation should be written without the aid of any illustrations.

TASK 7

Invent a machine of your own, using the same kind of style as Heath Robinson – it
does not have to be a serious invention which will go into production, but it should
be able to perform the function for which it is designed.

Draw an outline of your machine and write a caption of about ten words,
describing its purpose. The drawing should be detailed enough to enable pupils of
your own age to see how it works.

When it is finished, swap designs with a partner and write an explanation of how
your partner's machine works.

Evaluating explanations

Look at the following 'explanation' of the rules of cricket:

Explaining the 'Rules'
– not The Laws

You have two sides, one out in the field and one in. Each man that's in the side that's in goes out, and when he's out he comes in and the next man goes in until he's out.

When they are all out, the side that's out comes in, and the side that's been in goes out and tries to get those coming in out. Sometimes you get men still in and not out.

When both sides have been in and out, including the not outs, that's the end of the game.

TASK 8

a) Do you think the above is a good explanation? Ask yourself the following questions:
- does it make sense?
- is it concise?
- does it follow a logical sequence?
- if you knew nothing about the rules of cricket, would this help you to learn them?

b) From your answers to the above questions, you may come to the conclusion that this is not a very good explanation. Can you think of any other purpose for writing in such a way?

Hint: perhaps to entertain. If the purpose was to entertain, who do you think was the intended audience?

c) Think about, and write down, the ways in which it is not a good explanation.

d) Now choose a game that you know well. Write an explanation of how that game is played for someone with no knowledge of the rules.

Writing an explanation

Letters

Explanations, especially those given to large numbers of people, can often be delivered most effectively by using the form of a letter.

Read through the newspaper article below, which is based on actual events.

Parents protest as snow shuts school
Playground 'treacherous'

Angry parents demanded to know why hundreds of children were turned away from school this morning because the playground was covered in snow.

Hope Springs Junior and Infant School in Darkwood Road took the decision to close the doors on its 450 children this morning after arctic conditions left the playground covered under two inches of snow and ice.

Working parents complained that the decision to close the school, made at 8.25 this morning, gave them no time to make alternative arrangements for the care of their children. Many had to take the day off work.

Mrs Dawn Breaking, who has three children at the school, said: 'Surely it should have been possible for the school to cope with just two or three inches of snow? There was a heavier snowfall yesterday, and a path had been cleared and gritted before the children arrived. Why couldn't the caretaker have done the same this morning?

'I think it's disgraceful that our children's education is being disrupted in this way. If there had been no heating in the school I could understand it, but not just a little bit of snow in the playground.

'This has caused a great deal of trouble – most parents have to work and many can't afford to take time off.'

A spokesperson for Hope Springs Junior and Infant School told us that the school drive and playground were heavily frozen underneath the layer of snow.

Freezing weather

She said: 'Although the paths were cleared and gritted yesterday, the fresh snow and freezing weather had made it impossible to do the same this morning.

'The playground was in a very dangerous condition for the children. They could easily have slipped over and risked breaking their arms and legs.'

Layer of ice

A Brimington education spokesman said: 'The headteacher inspected the site early this morning and felt that it was in the best interests of pupils, parents and staff to close the school today.

'The playground was encased in a thick layer of ice – very much like a skating rink, which made all approaches to the school treacherous.'

Meanwhile, the local weather centre warned of more snow tonight, with temperatures set to plunge below minus four degrees centigrade. Motorists were advised not to undertake unnecessary journeys and council gritting machines and snowploughs have been put on red alert.

TASK 9

Imagine that you are the headteacher of Hope Springs School in Brimington. Following the events detailed in the newspaper report, you have decided to write a letter addressed to all the parents in your school, explaining why you made the decision to close on that day.

The newspaper article did not contain all the information which you had on the morning in question. Study the information below and opposite, and then write your letter. You will have to think carefully about the tone of your letter – it should be formal and polite. Remember, many parents were annoyed about the short notice of the school's temporary closure.

Weather Update for Thursday 14 January – heard on local radio at 6.05 a.m.

… and in the Brimington area, further snow showers, heavy at times, will continue throughout the day. Freezing temperatures, dipping to below -4° centigrade, could create problems on roads and motorways and drivers are warned to be extra cautious and to look out for patches of black ice.

MEMO

From: Brimington Chief Education Officer

To: All Brimington Primary & Secondary Headteachers

Concerning: Possible closure of schools in severe weather conditions

Date: 4 November

As we move towards the winter season, the following arrangements have been made regarding possible school closures.

Whenever severe weather conditions, such as heavy snow, occur, the Chief Education Officer, after consultation with the appropriate authorities, will make a decision as to whether or not **all** schools in Brimington will be closed.

If a decision to close is made, this will be broadcast on local radio as early as possible in order to allow parents time to make alternative care arrangements for their children.

However, individual headteachers still have the authority to close their school at any time if, in their opinion, there are health or safety considerations which apply.

FAX MESSAGE

FROM: COUNCIL EMERGENCY SNOW
HELPLINE

DATE: 14 JANUARY

TIME: 0645

TO: Ms B Wadsworth
Hope Springs J&I School

RE: REQUEST FOR GRITTING TEAM &
SNOWPLOUGH

Request is being processed.

Council gritting team will be at t[...]
school by 0730.

URGENT FAX MESSAGE

FROM: COUNCIL EMERGENCY SNOW
HELPLINE

DATE: 14 JANUARY

TIME: 0840

TO: Ms B Wadsworth
Hope Springs J&I School

RE: PREVIOUS REQUEST FOR GRITTING
TEAM & SNOWPLOUGH

Very much regret snowplough has
broken down en route. Will not be
possible to arrange alternative
today. Please accept our apologies.

Transcript of answerphone message received by Ms Wadsworth at 6.38 on Thursday morning.

HELLO MS WADSWORTH, THIS IS TONY ON MY MOBILE. I'M REALLY SORRY, BUT I WON'T BE IN SCHOOL THIS MORNING. I STARTED TO CLEAR A PATH ACROSS THE PLAYGROUND THIS MORNING, BUT I SLIPPED ON THE ICE AND I THINK I'VE BROKEN MY ARM. THE PLAYGROUND IS IN A REALLY DANGEROUS CONDITION WITH A THICK LAYER OF ICE UNDERNEATH THE SNOW COVERING. I'M NOT SURE, BUT I DON'T THINK YOU'LL BE ABLE TO CLEAR A SAFE WAY FOR THE PUPILS TO GET INTO THE SCHOOL THIS MORNING. I'LL HAVE TO GO NOW, THE AMBULANCE HAS JUST ARRIVED. BYE.

Using a logical sequence

The information on these two pages is taken from the book *Walking with Dinosaurs* by Tim Haines. It explains several theories as to why dinosaurs died out.

WS
19

TASK 10

a) The text, illustrations and captions have been jumbled together. Using clues from the text, decide in which order the separated paragraphs occur. Then, on two sides of A4, design a page using the whole text, including the photographs and captions.

b) One of the criteria by which the success of an explanation is judged at GCSE is how well the paragraphs within the explanation are linked. With this in mind, explain the reason for the position you have given each paragraph.

c) When you have completed the task, compare your version with the original in the book. Were there any differences? If so, why do you think these differences occurred. Is one version 'right' and one 'wrong'?

A

Finally, there was a big drop in sea levels and a 25 per cent increase in land surface. This was at the expense of the epicontinental seas and might have caused the fragmentation of animal populations.

B

One problem facing current analysis of the extinction is that the data is biased towards the western United States. The best and most detailed quantitative work has been done in places such as the Hell Creek Formation, which was a lush coastal plain in the Cretaceous. This area must have been subject to different stresses from those that occurred in places such as the desert of inland China, but comparative data does not exist.

C

D

For hundreds of thousands of years on either side of this event the movement of India up against the Asian continental plate produced massive, sustained volcanic activity. Now known as the Deccan Traps, this activity generated enough flood basalt to cover an area the size of Alaska and Texas together with lava almost 1 kilometre ($^1/_2$ mile) deep. This could have caused global cooling, and among the poisons ejected into the atmosphere would have been selenium, which is particularly toxic for developing embryos in eggs.

E
Research has revealed that there were at least three forces at work at the end of the Cretaceous, which would have made life pretty miserable for most organisms.

F
But extinction does not occur at an even rate. There appear to be quiet periods in the history of life, punctuated by 'mass' extinctions. In the past 550 million years there have been five major extinctions, when over 50 per cent of animal species died. The most significant of all was at the end of the Permian era, before the dinosaurs evolved – it wiped out 95 per cent of life. The most recent one occurred 65 million years ago and has attracted more attention than all the others because it finished off the dinosaurs.

G
A large crater in the Gulf of Mexico and a layer of the rare element iridium all round the world suggest that an asteroid or comet 10 kilometres (6 miles) wide hit Earth at this time. It could have caused severe acid rain, global wildfires and, as a layer of debris spread round the planet and blocked out the sun, a prolonged 'impact winter'.

H
Almost as infamous as dinosaurs themselves is the fact that they all died out in a very short space of time. To understand this event we have to put it in context. Extinction is an integral part of evolution – all creatures eventually die out and this does not imply 'failure'. Over 90 per cent of the organisms that have ever lived are extinct; evolution is a dynamic process and there is a constant turnover of species.

I
As this large hole in Arizona shows, meteors are enormously destructive. Al the end of the Mesozoic an object at least 10 kilometres (6 miles) wide crashed into the Gulf of Mexico, probably driving the dinosaurs to extinction.

J
Geologically active areas pour gases into the atmosphere, and at the end of the Mesozoic, as India collided with Asia, there was an enormous amount of volcanic activity. Some speculate that this is what killed off the dinosaurs.

K
There have been over 80 theories put forward to explain the demise of the dinosaurs. These include plague, constipation, mammals eating their eggs, racial senility, a nearby explosion of a supernova, being hunted down by aliens and many more. But any theory has to explain a very odd pattern of extinction. Herbivorous and carnivorous dinosaurs were badly affected, as were lizards, sharks, marsupials and a range of marine organisms. However, other mammals, crocodiles, turtles, frogs, salamanders and numerous other marine organisms survived relatively unscathed.

L

M
No single doomsday theory fits all the evidence, but since we know that all these events were taking place at the same time, it is possible that they all played a role in the mass destruction. Indeed, taken altogether, it is a wonder that anything at all survived.

Planning, organisation and communication

To gain the higher grades in your GCSE English, you will need to demonstrate the ability to:

- clearly identify the purpose and audience for which you are writing
- use a range of appropriate information
- organise that information into coherent paragraphs.

The first thing you must do for any given assignment is plan! Jotting ideas down on paper before you start to write is the initial step in the planning process. Once you have those ideas, you can begin to organise them into a coherent structure. When you have the ideas organised, you can begin to communicate the information to your audience.

TASK 11

Imagine that you are a teacher organising a field trip to a historical building thirty miles from the school, for a group of Year 10 pupils. The trip is part of their coursework requirement and you have to write a letter to the parents of the pupils involved to explain the purpose and organisation of the trip. You should write about 250 words.

You have jotted down the following points which you wish to include in the letter.

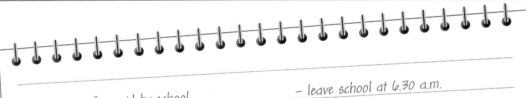

- entrance fee paid by school
- leave school at 6.30 a.m.
- Historic Windrick Castle and village
- waterproof clothing if rain
- return at 5.45 p.m. (approx.)
- opportunity for first-hand experience of medieval castle
- Date of visit: Thursday 23 June
- strong shoes/trainers needed (may get dirty)
- Larry's Luxury Coaches (used before – v. good!)
- voluntary contribution of £2 each needed to cover insurance and coach
- essential part of history coursework (10% of marks)
- packed lunch required
- some spending money (recommend no more than £3 – nothing to spend it on)
- Need parents' support with money
- possibility of joining archaeological dig on site (could be v. dirty!)

These notes form the basis of your plan. At present, the notes are in no particular order. You need to organise them into a coherent plan for a letter, using the following sequence:

- arrange the notes into appropriate groups of related subjects. For example, you could have a group entitled 'travel arrangements'
- once the ideas have been organised, add any other thoughts or ideas of your own which could be included in the letter
- you now need to put numbers next to the groups in the order you wish to include them in the letter. Think carefully about the beginning and ending of the letter – these are the areas which stand out.

When you have put your ideas in sequence, you can begin to communicate what you have to say by writing the letter. Remember, the main purpose of the letter is to explain, but you may feel it advisable to include some elements of information and persuasion. In particular, concentrate on:

- your audience – remember you are writing for adults
- the tone of your letter – you need to strike a careful balance between formality and friendliness
- links between paragraphs – to make the letter 'hang together' well
- appropriate and varied vocabulary to convince and interest the reader
- setting out the letter formally – use your own school address and remember to sign off 'Yours faithfully' if you begin with 'Dear Parent'.

Assessment – significant event

The following title is taken from a recent GCSE English paper.

Choose an event from your past that has particular significance for you. Explain what happened and your feelings about it.

Printed below is a student's attempt at answering this task. The first page has been marked by a GCSE examiner. Read it through and take note of the comments that the examiner has made.

Interesting opening sentence – gains reader's attention immediately.

Deliberate build up of tension – at this moment, the reader does not know <u>what</u> activity.

I had always regarded myself as someone who was good at sports. Not necessarily brilliant, but someone who picked up new games easily and who wasn't particularly tolerant of those who did not possess the same skills. I'm not being big-headed about this, but I'd represented the school at football, cricket, athletics and all the other sporting events that were on offer. It was against this background that I put my name down for a course of lessons at an activity centre on the outskirts of town, just a 15-minute drive away from the school. I didn't expect it would take long for me to master the basics and then progress quickly on to the advanced skills, and as I gazed around the other faces on the school mini bus as we drove to the centre, I couldn't help feeling a smug sense of pity for those less sporty individuals who would undoubtedly struggle in the sessions to come. It just shows how wrong you can be!

Opening paragraph sets the scene – prepares reader for what will happen later.

Effective last sentence. Reader is anticipating the next paragraph.

Good use of language – refers back to warnings in previous paragraph = coherent links.

Ten of us disembarked from the mini bus that <u>fateful afternoon</u>, and I felt a thrill of <u>anticipation</u> as I gazed up at the artificial mountain of the dry ski slope. We were taken into the centre and introduced to Pete, our instructor for the duration of the course. Boots and skis were distributed and I confidently strapped them on. I felt that in no time at all, I'd be riding the ski lift to the top and skiing <u>gracefully</u> down to stop with a flourish in front of an <u>admiring</u> crowd of onlookers. It was as I stood up and started to plod over to the beginners' slope that I began to get a sense of <u>foreboding</u>.

Conscious use of vocabulary to sha[...] the text.

Another coherent link between paragraphs.

<u>For a start</u>, the boots felt uncomfortable and different from how I had imagined them. They were stiff and unwieldy, and I kept slipping backwards when everyone else seemed to be gliding effortlessly along. I reassured myself that I'd soon get used to it once the expert instruction began. Wrong again!

Building up tensi[...] – by now, reader getting the idea t[...] the writer is not going to be succe[...] at skiing!

Here is the rest of the essay. Read it through and then outline the **qualities** and **weaknesses** of the response. In doing this you should refer to:

- awareness of audience
- tone and use of language
- paragraphing
- punctuation and spelling.

We were taken through our initial paces — how to hold the sticks, how to walk sideways up a slope, how to stand — and eventually Pete demonstrated how we were to ski down a gentle gradient and come to a controlled halt some ten metres further on. To my horror, I realised we would not all try this at once, where individual mistakes might be overlooked, but instead we would be skiing one at a time in front of the whole group. My sense of impending disaster was rapidly increasing.

Six fellow students were ahead of me, and they all (including a couple of the 'not-so-sporty' types mentioned previously) accomplished this relatively easy task with little difficulty. As my turn approached, I could feel the tension heighten in my legs and body and I was certain that this was not going to go smoothly. I knew what I wanted the skis to do but they seemed to have developed a life of their own. Sure enough, my worst fears were immediately realised. Whereas the others had sped straight down the slope, I lurched diagonally across it, away from Pete and my fellow skiers, and only managed to come to a halt because of the fence strategically placed to prevent non-skiers like me from appearing on the main road which runs past the centre. To their credit, none of my companions actually laughed out loud at my lack of expertise, but I could see in some of their faces the kind of smug superiority which I had often been guilty of when meeting players of lesser ability on the football field or cricket pitch. I felt even more uncomfortable, but this time it was because I was thinking about all the judgements I had passed on people during my sporting life.

The rest of the session passed in much the same way, with the others in the group gradually gaining in confidence and skill and progressing to the higher slopes. Me? I was kept behind on the lowest, most gentle slopes to practise the basics. To add to my humiliation, Pete kept using others in the group as examples of what I should be doing, and it was this aspect which had particular significance for me.

Previously, I had often been used as the example to show others how to do something correctly, but now the boot was well and truly on the other foot and I didn't like the experience at all. I began to see things, and myself, in a different light and I resolved there and then not to put other people under the judgemental spotlight that I had used before. Since my experience on the dry ski slopes, I have tried to be more sympathetic and helpful to others on and off the sports field. This isn't always easy because there is a delicate balance between being helpful and being patronising, but I have found that if you are genuinely trying to be helpful, then people usually recognise and accept this. I have also found that I am more ready to ask for and receive help and don't feel that it is a sign of weakness to accept that help. I can now look back and laugh at my first skiing experience and if ever I am tempted to judge other people's performances, I just have to remember the embarrassment I felt that day and I smile wryly and just mind my own business.

Unit 4 Instructions and advice

There are many similarities between instructions and advice. It can sometimes be difficult to determine which is which and sometimes, instructions and advice occur in the same piece of writing.

As a general rule, instructions are more direct and focused than advice. The writer *expects* the instruction to be carried out. For example, if you are loading a new game on your computer, it is important to follow the instructions carefully.

On the other hand, when advice is given, there is no requirement that it must be acted upon, only a *suggestion* that it could be. For example, once the new game has been loaded, you will want to learn how to play it: the game may come with tips or advice on good moves which will help you.

In this unit, you will be exploring in more detail the similarities and differences between instructions and advice. By looking at specific examples you will be able to distinguish between instructions and advice more easily and use them more effectively.

TASK 1

Look at the extract on the next page. It has been taken from an advice pack on household security, issued by the police.

The leaflet contains a mixture of advice and instructions.

Choose two examples of words or phrases which you think are examples of advice, and two which you think are examples of instructions. For each example say why you think it belongs to that category.

Compare your answers with a partner and discuss your reasons for putting the word or phrase into that particular category.

Around the home

Lighting

Good lighting can deter a thief.
Some exterior lights have an infra-red sensor that switches the light on for a few moments when it detects something in its range. Sensors can be bought separately to convert an existing outdoor light into a security one.

Look in when you're out

Most burglaries happen when a house or flat is empty, so:

- Use time switches – available from DIY shops – to turn on lights, radios and other appliances when you're out.

- Don't tempt the thief – keep all valuable items out of sight.

- Don't advertise your absence when you're on holiday, or even when out at work or shopping. Most burglars will only tackle an empty house.

- If you can, get a friend or neighbour to look after your home when you're away, by collecting your post, drawing your curtains at night and generally making the place look lived in. And be prepared to do the same for them.

Instructions

What are instructions?

Instructions are all around us – at home, at school and whenever we are out and about. Whether you are reading the label on a bottle of shampoo or simply waiting at a pelican crossing, you will find instructions telling you what to do.

Instructions are often known by other names, including rules, orders, directives and recipes. They are not written to persuade, nor are they written to argue a particular point of view; instead, they are written to tell us what we need to know to get somewhere or to do something and need to be expressed simply and clearly. Written and spoken instructions are often very different.

Look at the following transcript of a conversation. A is a driver who has stopped to ask the way to the local library. B is trying to give her directions.

B: OK, you go straight down this road until you come to a T-junction. You turn right and then drive along Billesley Lane until the roundabout. You take the, er ... second ... third ... fourth road off the roundabout. No, it's the third road ... it's kind of like a right turn but not quite ...

A: So it's the third exit?

B: Yeah, that's it. You take the third exit off the roundabout, then you go straight on until you see the bus garage on your left.

A: Right.

B: After that, turn right at the traffic lights ... Hang on a minute, there are two sets of lights. Yeah, you go straight through the first set and turn right at the second ... by the school.

A: Do you know the name of that road, or the school?

B: Yes, it's ... it's ... hang on a minute. Nah, it's gone, but anyway, you follow the main road for about half a mile, go under the railway bridge and then you'll find the library on the left ... just before McDonald's.

A: OK, thanks very much.

B: Marlow Road. That's it – I knew I'd remember. The library's on Marlow Road.

A: Thanks very much. Bye.

TASK 2

a) With a partner, discuss how clear these instructions are. The key question to ask is, 'Would the driver have been able to understand them and follow them to reach her destination?'

b) Using the above information, write out a set of clear, simple instructions which would give directions to the library.

c) Compare the two versions. What are the differences?

Obviously, the major difference between written and spoken instructions is that when writing instructions, you have more time to think about and plan what you write. In this way, you can avoid repetition and be sure about facts such as road names.

Use of imperatives

Look back at your finished written instructions from Task 2. Now underline all the verbs you can find. You will notice that they have been written almost like a set of commands, which is indeed what they are. Instead of writing, for example:

You take the third exit off the roundabout ...

you might have written:

Take the third exit off the roundabout. Or *Leave the roundabout by the third exit.*

In these examples, the subject (you) has been left out. The verbs 'Take' and 'Leave' have each been turned into a command or directive known as an imperative.

In the following examples of instructions, the imperative is in bold.
- **Walk** on the left.
- **Fill** in the form using black ink.
- **Insert** the disk into Drive A.

Always use imperatives when writing instructions.

Form

Instructions come in a wide variety of forms – such as recipes, advertisements, leaflets, manuals. To work out the form of a set of instructions, ask the question, 'what is it?'

TASK 3

a) Look again at the instructions you produced for Task 1. Under the heading 'Giving Directions', write down all the imperatives you used. Think of any other imperatives that you might use when asked to give directions, and add them to your list.

b) Write down the following headings, and under each one, try to list imperatives that are likely to be used when giving instructions. For example, *mix, pour* and *chop* are imperatives frequently used in recipes.
  - recipes
  - car manuals
  - DIY manuals
  - school rules.

Look at the examples of instructions below and then complete the task on the following page:

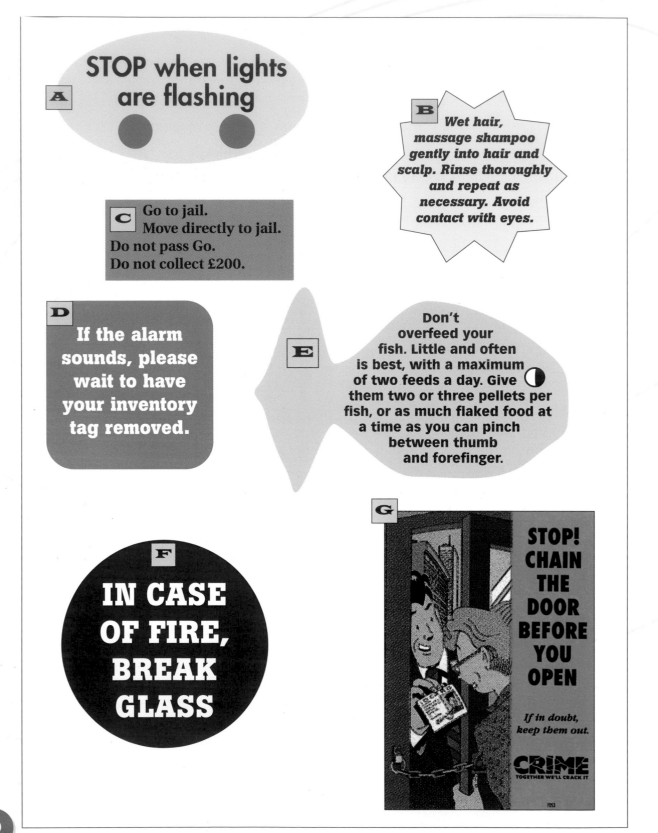

A STOP when lights are flashing

B *Wet hair, massage shampoo gently into hair and scalp. Rinse thoroughly and repeat as necessary. Avoid contact with eyes.*

C Go to jail. Move directly to jail. Do not pass Go. Do not collect £200.

D If the alarm sounds, please wait to have your inventory tag removed.

E Don't overfeed your fish. Little and often is best, with a maximum of two feeds a day. Give them two or three pellets per fish, or as much flaked food at a time as you can pinch between thumb and forefinger.

F IN CASE OF FIRE, BREAK GLASS

G STOP! CHAIN THE DOOR BEFORE YOU OPEN

If in doubt, keep them out.

CRIME
TOGETHER WE'LL CRACK IT

TASK 4

Copy out and complete the table below. For each set of instructions, write in:
- **What** it is (form), e.g. a leaflet, manual
- **Who** it was written for (its intended audience)
- **Where** you might find it.

The first one has been done for you.

	Form	Intended audience	Where found
A	Road sign	Road users	Side of the road
B			
C			
D			
E			
F			
G			

Features of written instructions

As you work through this unit, look out for the following features in the examples of instructions:
- clear and simple structures – the more complicated the instruction, the more difficult it will be to follow
- a logical, chronological order – obviously, the sequence of events is very important: if the sequence is wrong, the reader could easily become confused
- the use of simple language and short sentences which can be easily understood – to ensure that the instructions can be easily followed by the audience
- the lack of emotive language – trying to instruct, not to persuade or argue
- the use of directives (imperatives) to address the audience
- the use of the present tense, which gives a more immediate 'feel' to the instructions and helps to involve the audience.

Audience

In every type of writing, your audience – who you are writing for – is of great importance. Look carefully at the leaflets of instructions on these two pages, which are aimed at two different audiences, and then answer the questions which follow.

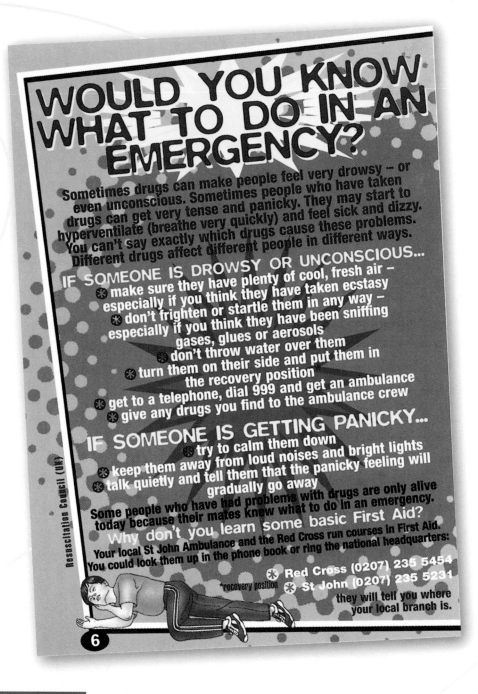

WOULD YOU KNOW WHAT TO DO IN AN EMERGENCY?

Sometimes drugs can make people feel very drowsy – or even unconscious. Sometimes people who have taken drugs can get very tense and panicky. They may start to hyperventilate (breathe very quickly) and feel sick and dizzy. You can't say exactly which drugs cause these problems. Different drugs affect different people in different ways.

IF SOMEONE IS DROWSY OR UNCONSCIOUS...
* make sure they have plenty of cool, fresh air – especially if you think they have taken ecstasy
* don't frighten or startle them in any way – especially if you think they have been sniffing gases, glues or aerosols
* don't throw water over them
* turn them on their side and put them in the recovery position*
* get to a telephone, dial 999 and get an ambulance
* give any drugs you find to the ambulance crew

IF SOMEONE IS GETTING PANICKY...
* try to calm them down
* keep them away from loud noises and bright lights
* talk quietly and tell them that the panicky feeling will gradually go away

Some people who have had problems with drugs are only alive today because their mates knew what to do in an emergency. Why don't you learn some basic First Aid? Your local St John Ambulance and the Red Cross run courses in First Aid. You could look them up in the phone book or ring the national headquarters:

*recovery position
* Red Cross (0207) 235 5454
* St John (0207) 235 5231
they will tell you where your local branch is.

Resuscitation Council (UK)

6

TASK 5

a) Who is the intended audience for each leaflet?

b) Explain how you were able to work out who the leaflets were aimed at – think in particular about:
* the language and vocabulary
* the subject matter
* sentence length
* illustrations.

Presentational features

Now look at the information on the opposite page, which shows you how to build an igloo. Some of the presentational features mentioned earlier are demonstrated.

> **Extra information and details** – although not all this information is instructional, it does give a background or context to the instructions which follow, and as such, makes the instructions easier to understand.

> **Heading and subheading in bold** – simple, self-explanatory titles, which reflect the subject matter and stand out.

> **Illustrations** – each stage of the process is accompanied by a colour illustration to aid the reader's understanding.

> **Numbers** – the process of building the igloo is shown chronologically – the instructions occur in the same order and the numbers ensure that the reader does not get confused.

> **Bold type and different coloured background** – highlights this vital health warning and ensures that the reader is aware of the danger.

> **Final illustration** – shows the reader what the final product should look like. There is also an unillustrated summary including extra information which could be helpful.

WS 25

TASK 6

a) Cover up the illustrations opposite and see if you could follow the written instructions alone. Do you think the illustrations make it easier or more difficult to carry out the instructions?

b) Cover up the words. Would it be easier or more difficult to carry out the task with illustrations alone?

c) Now, using both text and illustrations, write/draw a leaflet giving instructions for building a snowman. Use any presentational devices you think would be appropriate.

LIVING IN THE WILD

SNOW SHELTERS

PᴙovidED TEMPERATURES REMAIN below 0°C (32°F), constructing snow shelters is relatively easy. Sheltering from the wind is the first priority, since the wind can drastically decrease the air temperature *(see page 141)*. Temperatures below –10°C (14°F) become increasingly unpleasant, so that it becomes necessary to construct shelters in which heat can be retained extremely well. These can range from a simple, hollowed-out heap of snow to an igloo, which can take a few hours to construct. In a long-term shelter, such as an igloo, heavy, cold air can be diverted away from the occupants by digging a cold sink to channel the air down and away from the shelter. It is important to allow for adequate ventilation in all snow shelters in order to prevent suffocation.

BUILDING AN IGLOO

1 Cut blocks from dry, hard snow, using a snow saw or large knife. Each block should be about 1 m (3 ft) long, 40 cm (15 in) high, and 20 cm (8 in) deep.

2 Form a circle with blocks around the hole created where you cut the blocks. Cut the circle in a spiral from the top of the last block to the ground ahead of the first block. This will make it easy to construct a dome.

3 Build up the walls, overlapping the blocks and shaping them so that they lean inwards. Cut a hole under the wall for the cold sink and entrance. Put several blocks along one wall as a sleeping platform.

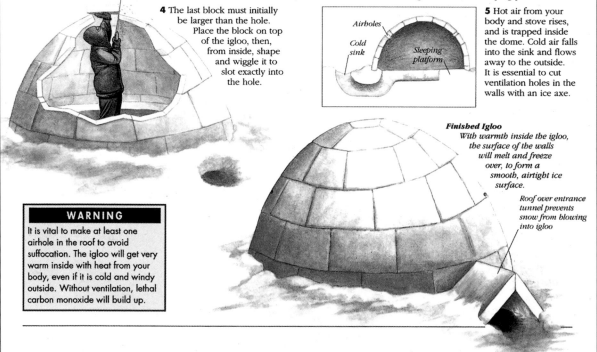

4 The last block must initially be larger than the hole. Place the block on top of the igloo, then, from inside, shape and wiggle it to slot exactly into the hole.

Airholes

Cold sink

Sleeping platform

5 Hot air from your body and stove rises, and is trapped inside the dome. Cold air falls into the sink and flows away to the outside. It is essential to cut ventilation holes in the walls with an ice axe.

Finished Igloo
With warmth inside the igloo, the surface of the walls will melt and freeze over, to form a smooth, airtight ice surface.

Roof over entrance tunnel prevents snow from blowing into igloo

WARNING

It is vital to make at least one airhole in the roof to avoid suffocation. The igloo will get very warm inside with heat from your body, even if it is cold and windy outside. Without ventilation, lethal carbon monoxide will build up.

Outdoor Survival Guide by Hugh McManners

Assessment – recipes

A recipe is a type of instruction which often has its own specific structure and language. Look at the recipe below, which comes from a book aimed at students.

Name of dish

Sun-dried Tomato and Herb Omelette

Preparation time: 5 minutes + 5 minutes cooking. Freezing: not recommended. Serves 1

Information on preparation time and how many the meal serves

More information regarding the dish, to give a context

An omelette is one of the quickest vegetarian dishes. You can vary the flavouring according to your taste, and to what is available.

2 medium eggs

4 sun-dried tomatoes in oil, drained

2 tablespoons chopped fresh herbs, such as chervil, chives and parsley

15 g (1/2 oz) butter

salt and freshly ground black pepper

Ingredients – what is needed to make the dish and the quantities required

Main instructions – numbered to reinforce the sequential nature of the task

1 Break the eggs into a bowl and beat them lightly until just combined. Chop the sun-dried tomatoes and add to the eggs, together with the herbs. Season with salt and pepper.

2 Put a 15-cm (6-inch) frying-pan over a medium heat. When it is hot add the butter, turn the heat up and swirl the butter around – don't let it brown.

3 Pour in the eggs, tilting the pan to distribute them evenly, then, using a fork, draw the set edges towards the centre and let the liquid egg run to the edges. Repeat until the omelette is almost set.

4 Tilt the pan over a warmed plate, then fold the edge of the omelette over to the centre and let it fold over again on to the plate. Serve immediately.

Photo of finished product – the reader knows what their dish will look like

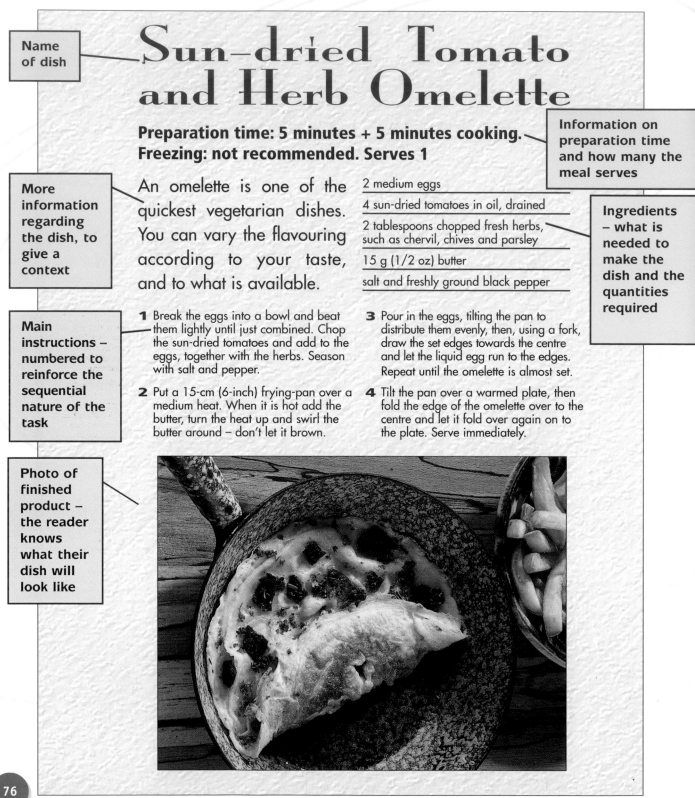

Sainsbury's Quick and Easy Vegetarian Meals for Students by Rose Elliot

Now look at two slightly different recipes. These date from the seventeenth century, and were supposed to cure victims of the bubonic plague, or Black Death as it was known. The cause of the disease was not known at the time and these remedies would have had no effect on the poor victims.

More recipes against the Plague

1

Take three pints of muscadine wine, boil it in a handful of Sage, as much rue, till a pint is wasted, then strain it, and set it on ye fire again, then put therein of long pepper, ginger and nutmegs, of each ye 3rd part of an ounce, beat all together into a fine powder, let it boil a little, then put therein 2 ounces of treacle, an ounce of Metrodate, and a quarter of a pint of Angelico water before you put them in. Take of it warm both morning and evening in your bed a spoonful or two, if infected, and sweat after it, but if not infected a spoonful a day is sufficient, half in ye morning, and half in ye evening, to prevent infection.

2

Take the inward Bark of the Ash Tree one Pound, of Walnut, with the green outward Shells, to the number of Fifty, cut these small: of Scabious, of Vervin, of each a handful, of Saffron two Drams, pour upon these the strongest Vinegar you can get, four Pints, let them a little boil together upon a very soft fire, and then stand in a close Pot, well stopt all night upon the embers. After distil them with a soft fire, and receive the Water close Kept. Give unto the Patient laid in Bed and well covered with Cloathes, two ounces of this water to drink, and let him be provoked to Sweat: and every eight hours (during the space of four and twenty Hours) give him the same quantity to drink.

TASK 7

a) Read carefully through the recipes above. There are differences in the way words are spelled, and in the way sentences are structured, which make the language a little difficult to understand in places. With a partner, discuss each recipe and try to work out what is being said.

b) When you have done this, choose one of the recipes and re-write it in modern English, including, perhaps, an illustration of what the finished product should look like. (I'll leave this to your imagination!)

Use the layout on the previous page to help you.

Advice

Walk into any careers advice centre, public library, police station or doctor's surgery and you will immediately be surrounded by posters, leaflets and pamphlets, all giving helpful advice on a wide range of topics.

Written advice contains many of the features used in written instructions (see page 71), often including:

- clear and simple structures
- a logical, chronological order
- the use of the present tense.

Advice often uses imperatives (though less than in written instructions) to make points more strongly.

However, there are some features which help to distinguish advice from instructions. The main differences are that advice often:

- contains more information
- *recommends* a course of action to the reader, rather than *directs* the reader to follow that course
- gives reasons for any recommendation
- suggests different options, so the reader has a choice in what they do
- is written in a more informal tone.

TASK 8

The following extract gives advice for travellers to Barbados. Read it carefully and try to identify as many as you can of the features listed opposite.

Health

Travelling in Barbados is usually very safe as far as health is concerned. Food is invariably well and hygienically prepared, and the tapwater, drawn from springs and rain filtered by the island's coral, is safe to drink.

No jabs are needed – the major tropical diseases were eradicated long ago – and you'll find that the only real threat to your physical welfare is the intense **Caribbean sun**. Many visitors get badly sunburned on the first day and suffer for the rest of the trip – you'll see them peeling around the island. To avoid their fate, it's advisable to wear a strong sunscreen at all times; if you're after a tan, start strong and gradually reduce the factor. As for exposure times, fifteen minutes a day in the early morning or late afternoon is recommended, if rarely followed; unreconstructed sunworshippers should at least avoid the heat of the day between 11.30am and 2.30pm. For the sunburned, aloe vera gel is available at the island's pharmacies.

While you're on the beach, steer clear of the **manchineel trees**, recognizable by their shiny green leaves and the small, crab apple-like fruits that will be scattered around. The fruit is poisonous and, when it rains, the bark gives off a poisonous sap which will cause blisters if it drips on you. The sea, too, poses a handful of threats. Don't worry about the rarely seen sharks or barracudas, which won't spoil your visit, but watch out for spiny black **sea urchins**. They're easily missed if you're walking over a patch of sea grass; if you step on one and can't get the spines out, you'll need medical help.

Barbados Mini Rough Guide by Adam Vaitilingam

Read through the following article, which gives you information on what and how to eat and drink when hiking through snow.

Backcountry Food and Water

By Teri Matthews

The exposure to cold, mixed with the physical exertion of backcountry travel, depletes the body of energy and water quickly. Without rehydrating and replacing energy, the human body lacks the ability to transport oxygen and nutrients to the muscles, through the blood.

The reason people become tired right after eating, is because blood is also used in the intestines to help digestion. By eating small amounts throughout the trip and continuously drinking fluids, muscles can continue steadily without complete burnout. Besides, trying to stuff yourself after a long hard day may produce indigestion and fatigue that last for several hours.

Bring foods that you enjoy, because extended hiking at altitude can reduce the appetite. Taking a variety of food will help the body utilize different nutrients, increasing energy. Many athletes look down on sugar because it gives a quick energy boost, as opposed to complex carbohydrates which provide long-lasting energy. Some candy is fine, but be sure to mix it with more nutritious foods. Lightweight items, that will not turn to pulp, are the best. A smashed banana in the pack is not quickly forgotten.

Although many people prefer a hot meal, it is better to have items that don't require cooking during the day. Even at night there are times when it's too late, too windy, or you're too tired to cook. Besides, you still have to melt and boil snow for hot drinks, as well as for water the next day. Dried fruits, nuts, cheese, beef jerky, canned meat, sausage, crackers, bagels, chocolate, candy and energy bars are among favourites. Dehydrated pastas, soups, tea, cocoa and packets of oatmeal are also easy to prepare and clean up. My favourite items are oranges, fruit bars, hot pepper cheese and Stouffers boil in a bag meals. (These items are fairly heavy but good for short trips.) Bring enough stove fuel for increased cooking times at altitude and pack extra food in case of an emergency.

If you are thirsty, you are already dehydrated. The recommendation for the average person to replenish water, after intense activity, is two quarts. For hot environments, four quarts. Salt replenishment is also important. Tablets of salt or powdered drink mixes canbe used for sodium replacement. Carry a water bottle, canteen or camel back and continuously drink water all day to keep the system running smoothly. It's just like a car needing the right amount of oil. If there is not a lot of fluid in the stomach, digestion of food is much faster. So, drinking a little at a time all day, instead of just during a meal is more efficient.

When preparing to refill water bottles by melting snow, it is faster to start with some water each time and use dense snow because it has a higher water content. If using water out of the creek, or anywhere Ghiardia may be found from human or animal waste, it is essential to use purification tablets or filters. Boiling the water for ten minutes, or more at high altitude will also kill the bacteria, but other methods are usually convenient. Once the bottles are filled for the next day, put it beside your body that night so it will not freeze.

For optimal performance eat and drink small quantities throughout the entire day. Carry a variety of foods you really like, that are easy to prepare and high in long-lasting energy. Then think of rehydration as the source of blood, supplying the muscles with much needed fuel to go bigger, faster, and higher. important.

TASK 9

The article above contains many **recommendations**, together with background information which enables the reader to understand the **reasons** for those recommendations. For example,

> *Bring foods that you enjoy* (recommendation)
> *because extended hiking at altitude can reduce the appetite* (reason).

Make a table like the one below.

Recommendations	Reasons (main points only)

In the left-hand column, note down the recommendations that the author makes. In the right-hand column, note the reasons that he gives for his recommendations. (Don't copy out large chunks of text; you should pick out the main points in note form.)

Assessment – football

Read the following two pages, which come from *Shoot*, a football magazine. Then complete Tasks 11 and 12, which are printed at the bottom of this page and the next.

TASK 11 – READING

a) In the article, much advice is given on how to become a football star. Summarise this advice in about 75 words.

b) The tone of the article is quite informal and friendly. How is this achieved? Write about 75–100 words.

c) Briefly describe the presentation of the pages, and explain why you think this presentation is effective (or ineffective).

TIM FLOWERS
(LEICESTER CITY)
"Just try as hard as you can and be prepared to make a few sacrifices. You'll see all your mates going out on a Saturday, chatting up loads of girls, but if you want to make it, you have to look after your body. It's worth it because the rewards are great."

MARTIN GRAINGER
(BIRMINGHAM)
"Look after yourself, eat the right things and take care of your body. If you stay dedicated and work hard, you can achieve what you want."

LEE SHARPE (BRADFORD)
"Just try and enjoy your football. If you're not happy playing the game, you won't improve and you might as well give up now. Also, it's very important to never stop believing."

CHRIS SUTTON (CHELSEA)
"There's a good chance you'll get spotted if you're playing for your local team. There's always scouts at these events, and although one or two players do slip through the net, most players, who are good enough, do get noticed. So if you want to reach the top, make sure you join your local team, and get loads of practise. The more you go through the basics of the game, the better you'll get."

ADE AKINBIYI (WOLVES)
"One really important part of being a successful footballer is training. When I was young, the manager judged me on my training, and not how well I played the matches. And if you're a youngster who wants to break into a side, that's how you prove yourself. So if you want to make it, remember one thing - it doesn't matter how tired you are or how cold it is, you have to learn to enjoy training if you want to reach the top."

WORK AT Shoot
SHOOT is always on the look out for bright, talented young people to take on a one or two week work placement at our office in London. If you're interested in a career in football journalism or magazine design, why not drop us a line? Address your letters to: Andrew Winter (Editor), SHOOT, IPC Magazines, King's Reach Tower, Stamford Street, London SE1 9LS.

TASK 12 – WRITING

You are the manager of an under-12 football team. You have read the article, and want to present a newsletter to the players, giving them advice on how to 'make it to the top'. You should write about 150 words.

REMEMBER

- **use your summary** to help you, but put your points together in a logical order; for instance, you might group health/fitness issues together
- think about what **presentational devices** you might use, such as bullet points, paragraphing and so on
- express yourself in **clear English**.

Printed below is a student's attempt at answering Task 11. It has been marked by a GCSE examiner. Read it through, and take note of comments that the examiner has made.

a) There is a lot of advice given. One thing is that you should keep your body healthy and enjoy it. If you do that, you'll have a chance of going far in the game. Make sure to train and it'll all come together. Another thing is to play for your local team. There's always scouts at those events, and although one or two players slip through the net, most players who are good enough do get noticed. Also you should attend a soccer school to develop your skills. They are good fun and you learn a lot.

There were about nine or ten different points that should have been made here, yet the candidate has simply picked three of them, and ignored all the others. Also, large chunks of the passage have been copied out. In doing this, the candidate has gone over the word limit.

[Remember, you demonstrate your understanding by completing the task set within the word limit.]

b) The tone is friendly because the players are smiling in the pictures, and they are telling the readers about what they did when they were kids.

I expected comments on language here — use of 'you' to give the impression of speaking directly to the reader, and informal, friendly tone.

c) The layout is really good and the writer must be very pleased. There are lots of quotes in boxes and that is good, and there are star players that kids like to read about. It is effective because people will buy the magazine.

Again, I would have expected to see comments about layout, colour, use of star players, etc. Also, the second part of the question has been misunderstood, and the candidate does not begin to explain why the layout would be <u>effective</u>.

Examiner's comments

The candidate has made some attempts to respond to the text, but unfortunately, hasn't shown a clear understanding of the text or what was expected. Copying out sections of text will never earn any marks, especially when the question demands that you 'summarise' — select the main points from the whole document, in this case. Also, this candidate doesn't seem to know what sorts of things candidates are expected to refer to — for instance, an understanding of basic presentational devices used in the media.

Altogether, the work would be unlikely to achieve even the lowest GCSE grade.

TASK 13

Here is a student's attempt at answering Task 11. Read it through, and then outline the **qualities** and **weaknesses** of the response. In doing so, you should refer to:

- content
- organisation
- use of presentational devices
- clarity of written English
- punctuation and spelling.

WS
29

> So you want to make it to the top?
> Take some advice.

1) Work hard at your game remember the more you train the more you learn about the game

2) Live a healthy lifestile this means eating well.

3) Enjoy the game for if you don't enjoy it you wont improve

4) Make sure that you keep your body healthy.

5) When your training always take advise, listen to people because you never stop learning.

6) Play for your local team as that is where you'll be spotted.

7) Go to soccer schools that's where you get good advice from people who know what their doing.

> Follow this advice and you
> won't go far wrong.
> Remember, you have to be strong.
> Be strong physcally.
> Be strong mentally.

Unit 5 Persuasion

Have you read a magazine or newspaper today?
Have you watched any television?
Have you listened to local radio?
Have you connected to the Internet?
Have you glanced at any advertising hoardings on your way to school?

If the answer to any of these questions is 'yes', then the chances are that you have been influenced by the power of persuasion.

Every day, and in almost every aspect of our lives, you are exposed to texts which attempt to influence the way you think and act. Advertisements try to persuade you to buy a particular product, politicians try to persuade you to vote for them and friends may try to persuade you to go somewhere or do something.

Persuasion can sometimes be very obvious – for example, a small child trying to persuade a parent to let them stay up late – but at other times it can be very subtle and almost undetectable. Occasionally, people can be persuaded by a forceful salesperson or a particularly effective advert into buying things that they do not need or cannot afford.

In order to be able to make informed choices without being unduly influenced by various types of persuasion, both subtle and not so subtle, you need to be able to recognise the various types which you might meet.

TASK 1

Copy out and then complete the table below. List all the things you have read, seen or heard in the last two days which have involved persuasion. (This could include examples where you have done the persuading!)

An example has been included to start you off.

Form of persuasion	Purpose	Result/effect
Discussion with mum	To persuade her to give me some money towards a new computer game	I didn't get the money (or the game!)

Analysing persuasive texts

Persuasive writing can appear in many forms, including letters, leaflets, brochures and, of course, advertisements. It is important to be able to detect who the text is aimed at – its audience – and why it has been written – its purpose. You may think the purpose is obvious, that is, to persuade, but you need to recognise the *specific reason* – is to change your opinion? To induce you to buy a particular product? To encourage you to act or behave in a different way?

TASK 2

Look at the examples on the next few pages. For each one, answer the following questions, giving reasons for your views:

a) What do you think the text comes from? (form)

b) Who is it aimed at? (audience)

c) What is it trying to persuade you to do or think?

d) What are the differences from and/or similarities with the others?

Baby for Adoption

Whisky is a lively five year old who lives with his mother Happy Dragon off the coast of the Moray Firth in Scotland. Traditionally, he would have a long, carefree life ahead of him with few natural dangers. A life full of friendship, fun and freedom to follow his natural instincts - exactly what any parent would want for their child. Unfortunately, today, many dolphins like Whisky are threatened daily by pollution, over-fishing, capture and drowning in fishing nets.

Adopt a Dolphin

That is why the Whale & Dolphin Conservation Society (WDCS) is asking you to adopt Whisky, or his friend Sundance, for just £3 a month. By doing so, you will be helping our fight to protect all whales and dolphins.

Return your form today and you will receive an adoption pack to introduce you to your chosen dolphin. You will also get regular mailings - our six-monthly full colour WDCS Magazine, plus six-monthly newsletters - as well as our video, 'The World of Whales and Dolphins'. Junior adopters will receive two editions of our 8 page junior magazine throughout the year.

Send for your adoption pack today and start working with us to protect dolphins like Whisky in their natural environment. Spread the cost of your adoption by using the direct debit form below - it's easy for you and saves our administration costs.

Patron:
Her Majesty The Queen

President:
Her Royal Highness, Princess Alexandra, G.C.V.O.

Chairman of the Council:
Professor R.D.Cohen, C.B.E., M.D., F.R.C.P.

Director-General:
Sir Paul Nurse, F.R.S., Hon. F.R.C.P.

Registered Charity No. 209631

61 Lincoln's Inn Fields, London WC2A 3PX

Tel: 020 7269 3662, Fax: 020 7269 2865

Imperial Cancer Research Fund

Please support Imperial Cancer Research Fund's 2000 Appeal in Birmingham by sending £2 a month

Dear Householder,

I very much hope that you can spare £2 a month to bring hope to everyone touched by cancer.

Finding new answers in the prevention, treatment and cure of cancer is a challenge that belongs to all of us. Because the sad fact is, two in five of us will get cancer at some point in our lives.

But we have made several important advances recently and are on the brink of many more. In fact, we believe that many thousands more lives could be saved if we can continue with our research into cancer. But long term research needs long term funding.

Please help us plan ahead, by sending £2 a month to support Imperial Cancer Research Fund's 2000 Appeal in Birmingham.

We are determined to help more and more people survive cancer. We're working with doctors and scientists all over the world, sharing our discoveries to advance our understanding of this disease. Will you play your part too, by supporting Imperial Cancer Research Fund's 2000 Appeal in Birmingham?

Thanks to the generous support of people like you, we're already making significant progress. There is still a long way to go, but just look at some of the advances that have been announced in recent months, none of which would have happened without donations from people like you:

Turning science into hope

0045755/6

A closer look . . .

When analysing persuasive texts, you should bear in mind the following:

- language
- structure
- style
- presentation.

TASK 3

Study the following extract, which comes from a brochure for the Millennium Dome. Some of the persuasive techniques used in the text and the photograph have been written in. Place each of the points made round the outside of the extract under one of the four headings above.

emotive language to highlight the achievement that is the Dome [awesome, exciting, inspiring, unforgettable, spectacular, amazing].

1

repetition (of 'A time ...') – a well known stylistic device to make sure the message gets across forcibly (points like this are often used in threes)

2

short sentences for effect – move you along quickly

3

use of imperatives – instructing the reader

4

personal appeal to reader by including us in the text – 'you', 'your' and 'we': the reader feels directly involved

5

involvement again of the reader – this time it implies that we have helped to build the Dome!

6

logo – to form an association with the event

7

One amaz

The year 2000 is special — and so is everyone who'll experience it. It's a unique moment in history: the dawn of a new millennium. A time of religious importance. A time to remember for the rest of your life. A time to enjoy the most amazing day out ever.

The Dome is unlike anywhere you've been before — an awesome space, full of exciting, inspiring things to see and do. It's your chance to embark on an unforgettable journey into the future. Marvel at a spectacular live performance. Reflect on the issues that will shape the new millennium. And simply have the time of your life.

The Millennium Experience at the Dome will have a profound and lasting effect on everyone who visits. It's something that will be talked about for years to come. An achievement that the rest of the world is looking on with envy and admiration. Together we've built something to be truly proud of. So enjoy this whirlwind tour of the Dome. However amazing it looks, the reality is even better...

8 large font and use of colour to make headline stand out

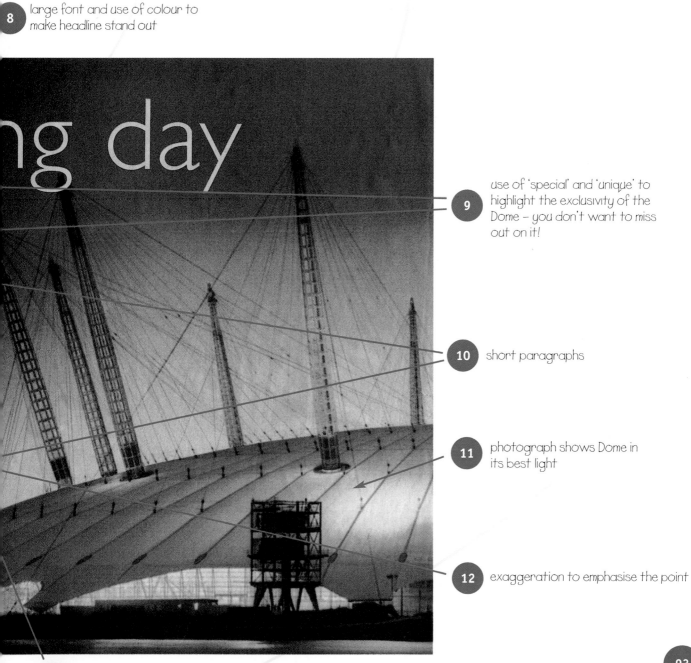

ng day

9 use of 'special' and 'unique' to highlight the exclusivity of the Dome – you don't want to miss out on it!

10 short paragraphs

11 photograph shows Dome in its best light

12 exaggeration to emphasise the point

13 positive statement on the outcome of your visit

On this page and the next is some information from the brochure for the Millennium Dome. The heading, the twelve paragraphs and the illustrations have been numbered. Study the information carefully and then do Tasks 4 and 5.

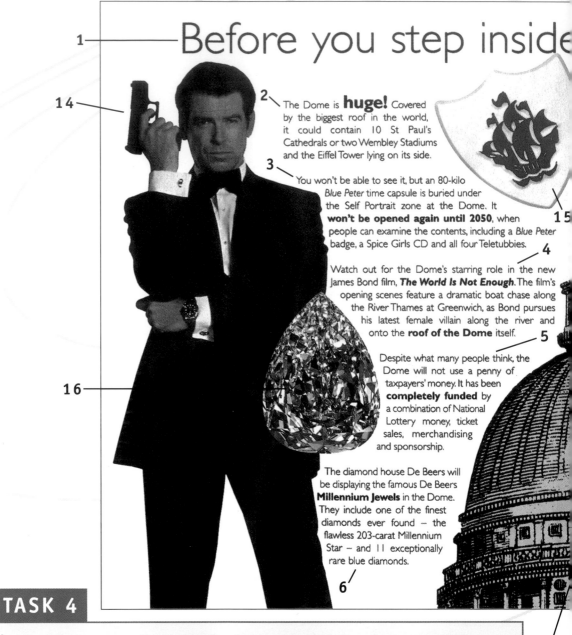

1 — # Before you step inside

2 — The Dome is **huge!** Covered by the biggest roof in the world, it could contain 10 St Paul's Cathedrals or two Wembley Stadiums and the Eiffel Tower lying on its side.

3 — You won't be able to see it, but an 80-kilo *Blue Peter* time capsule is buried under the Self Portrait zone at the Dome. It **won't be opened again until 2050**, when people can examine the contents, including a *Blue Peter* badge, a Spice Girls CD and all four Teletubbies.

4 — Watch out for the Dome's starring role in the new James Bond film, **The World Is Not Enough**. The film's opening scenes feature a dramatic boat chase along the River Thames at Greenwich, as Bond pursues his latest female villain along the river and onto the **roof of the Dome** itself.

5 — Despite what many people think, the Dome will not use a penny of taxpayers' money. It has been **completely funded** by a combination of National Lottery money, ticket sales, merchandising and sponsorship.

The diamond house De Beers will be displaying the famous De Beers **Millennium Jewels** in the Dome. They include one of the finest diamonds ever found – the flawless 203-carat Millennium Star – and 11 exceptionally rare blue diamonds.

6

14

15

16

17

TASK 4

a) For each item, say why you think it has been included on these pages and explain any features of language, structure, style or presentation that you find.

b) When you have identified these features, group the paragraphs and illustrations together under the following headings:
   - emotive language
   - green issues
   - use of celebrities
   - use of artwork/illustrations
   - general interest.

do your Domework...

7 Although the Dome itself is built to last for years, the Millennium Experience inside will be open for **just one year**. So if you don't manage to catch it
8 before 31 December 2000, you've missed out for ever.

Fifteen acres of land around the Dome have been replanted and will mature into **a living legacy** of dry meadowlands, parkland and wetlands. Along the river bank
9 new habitats for animals, fish and birds have been created.

Rainwater will be collected from the Dome roof, filtered and purified, then used to **flush the visitors' toilets** – an estimated 30 million flushes a year!
10

Every visitor to the Dome will receive a free copy of the **Dome's own newspaper**, *The Daily Dome*. The newspaper will be produced every day of the year for one year only, exclusively for visitors. As well as featuring national and international news, it will also include a Dome diary and an **essential guide** to the zones and key attractions.
11

Some of the biggest names in the arts world have worked on the Dome, including film producer **David Puttnam**, architects **Zaha Hadid** and **Richard Rogers**, sculptors **Antony Gormley** and **Ron Mueck** and cartoonist **Gerald Scarfe**, whose 3D caricatures can be seen in the Self Portrait zone. There's even an official poet-in-residence, **Simon Armitage**.
12

Visitors to the Dome are expected to drink 137,362 **cups of tea** a day.

A Royal Mint press in the Dome will make special **millennium crowns** (face value £5) for sale to visitors.
13

18

DECEMBER

3I

FRIDAY

19

20

TASK 5

a) Who do you think is the intended audience for these pages?

b) What is your personal opinion of the effectiveness of these pages? Explain why you think this.

c) Has this brochure persuaded you to want to visit the Dome? Why, or why not?

The reality ...

The Millennium Dome opened in late December 1999 in a huge blaze of publicity — some of it good, some of it bad. In January, the *Daily Mail* ran the following story about an advertisement for the Dome which they thought was misleading the public. Read through the article carefully, then do the tasks on the next page.

The truth zone

Dome ad campaign 'misleads the public'

By MATTHEW HICKLEY
Home Affairs Reporter

MILLENNIUM Dome chiefs have been accused of misleading the public with an advertisement campaign which appears to feature rave reviews from national newspapers.

Most of the 'reviews' consist of a few words lifted from articles published long before the Dome opened. Some are taken completely out of context.

Critics accused the Dome's operator the New Millennium Experience Company of using 'half-truths' to boost flagging ticket sales for the £758million attraction. The NMEC is under pressure to attract 12million visitors to Greenwich by the end of the year.

The Press advertisements, part of a multi-million-pound campaign which also includes lavish television slots, feature a five-year-old boy actor gazing in wonder at the Body Zone.

Unsurprisingly there is no mention of the two-hour queues which have snaked around the giant pink body sculpture on busy days.

Slogans are splashed across the advertisement, apparently informing would-be visitors what papers think of the Dome. The Daily Mail is quoted as calling it: 'A huge musical and visual extravaganza.'

While these words did appear in the Mail, they were not a review of the attraction itself. In fact they described what was expected of the opening night gala celebrations - in an article printed before the Dome opened.

A quotation from the Daily Telegraph - 'A Dome full of fun' - misses out the first half of the sentence which actually read: 'Trite, glitch-ridden, but a Dome full of fun.'

The only paper to be quoted accurately is the Mirror.

The NMEC's chief spokesman Jez Sagar defended the advertisements. 'It's a technique, ' he said. 'It is something that the entertainment industry does. You always see the big words outside the theatres in the West End, and this advertisement follows the same approach.'

Tory culture spokesman Peter Ainsworth said: 'This entire project has been marked by a lack of candour and straight dealing.

'Now we find that the advertising campaign is based on half-truths and quotations taken out of context.

'There is no point in luring people to the Dome under false pretences. NMEC should be straightforward about what is there, and who has said what about it.'

An advertising industry source said it was 'very naive' to make claims which might be proved false, leaving the NMEC vulnerable to complaints to the Advertising Standards Authority.

With daily attendance figures hovering well below the 10,000 mark last week, the NMEC is pinning its hopes on a massive surge in ticket sales during the summer, when it expects millions of foreign tourists to swell the ranks of visitors. On 140 days during school holidays the Dome will open for 'double sessions', and executives believe up to 50,000 people a day will go.

The Dome must still attract an average of more than 22,000 visitors a day for the rest of the year. So far, only 20,000 tickets are available each day.

Last week the NMEC hurriedly scrapped rules barring the public from buying tickets on the door, although officials still refuse to reveal how many tickets are being sold.

Even if the target of 12million visitors does prove optimistic, NMEC could avoid financial embarrassment by selling the site at the end of the year.

While the official budget estimates income from the sale would only be £15million, offers are thought to be nearer the £100million mark.

Details of six shortlisted bidders are expected this week. The Government will announce the winner in the summer.

The truth zone

The Independent
ADVERT: 'The biggest and best show on earth'
What the newspaper really said: On December 13, more than a fortnight before the Dome opened, an article ended with the sentence: 'Roll up for the biggest and best show on earth.' It was not a review. The author had just visited what was still a building site and had admitted he had not seen a single zone.

The Sun
ADVERT: 'One of the wonders of the world'
What the newspaper really said: The quote is not from a review of the Dome. In a leading article written weeks before the Dome opened, the *Sun* said: 'People will flock to visit (the Dome). We should all be jumping with excitement that we've got one of the wonders of the world on our doorstep.'
Since opening night, the *Sun* has toned down its enthusiasm. Last week the paper claimed that Dome staff were being sent home early because so few people were 'flocking to visit' the site.

The Daily Telegraph
ADVERT: 'A Dome full of fun'
What the newspaper really said: 'Trite, glitch-ridden, but a Dome full of fun,' – a headline on December 20, ten days before the Dome opened. The review was mixed, praising a few attractions, but adding pointedly: 'Far too many of the 10 Dome zones open yesterday were deathly dull in their didacticism, treating their audiences like idiots.'
A subsequent leading article said the Dome had 'got off to a poor start, and it is pointless for those who carry responsibility for it, such as Lord Falconer and its chief executive, Jennie Page, to pretend otherwise'.

Daily Mail
ADVERT: 'A huge musical and visual extravaganza'
What the newspaper really said: On December 11, almost three weeks before the Dome opened, the *Mail* reported that the Beatles song *Let It Be* would be performed inside the Dome on New Year's Eve as 'the finale to a huge musical and visual extravaganza watched by the Queen and some 10,000 guests'. Far from being a review of the Dome, the report made no mention of the daily shows now being seen by paying visitors.

The Mirror
ADVERT: 'A massive hit'
What the newspaper really said: Here, for once, the advert is accurate. The *Mirror* used the description in an article a few days after the Dome opened. More recently, however, the *Mirror* has been less enthusiastic, devoting considerable space to reporting dismally low attendance figures and to suggesting improvements.

TASK 6

a) Do you think the Dome advertisements mentioned in this article would have misled people?

b) This is a persuasive article written by a *Daily Mail* journalist. What do you think is the writer's view on the Dome?

c) What persuasive techniques has the journalist used in this article?

TASK 7

Now, write a leaflet which persuades people to visit your school. Use a range of persuasive techniques to make the leaflet attractive to an audience of parents and mature members of the school.

Getting the tone right

There are many occasions when letters are used to try to persuade. These can range from a begging letter asking for money to a letter of application for a job.

You will need to adopt an appropriate tone and style depending on your audience – will your letter be formal or informal? Will you have headings and/or subheadings?

You will also have to ensure that your letter is accurately written, grammatically correct and contains the appropriate punctuation. You could still use persuasive techniques such as emotive language or headings, but probably not to the same extent as you would in a leaflet or brochure. A firm receiving an application letter might not look favourably on one which starts with the headline IDEAL CANDIDATE FOR JOB – EMPLOY NOW!

Most pupils have a Work Experience placement in Year 10 or 11. Imagine the following information appeared on the notice-board at your school.

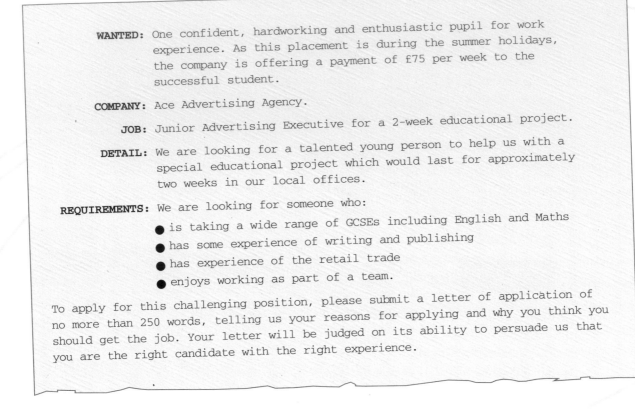

WANTED: One confident, hardworking and enthusiastic pupil for work experience. As this placement is during the summer holidays, the company is offering a payment of £75 per week to the successful student.

COMPANY: Ace Advertising Agency.

JOB: Junior Advertising Executive for a 2-week educational project.

DETAIL: We are looking for a talented young person to help us with a special educational project which would last for approximately two weeks in our local offices.

REQUIREMENTS: We are looking for someone who:
- is taking a wide range of GCSEs including English and Maths
- has some experience of writing and publishing
- has experience of the retail trade
- enjoys working as part of a team.

To apply for this challenging position, please submit a letter of application of no more than 250 words, telling us your reasons for applying and why you think you should get the job. Your letter will be judged on its ability to persuade us that you are the right candidate with the right experience.

Out of the fifty or so replies received by the company, there were three which stood out. These three letters are reproduced on the following pages.

TASK 8

Imagine that you and a partner are the selection team for the placement at Ace Advertising. Your job is to read through these applications carefully and choose who should get the job.
- Discuss the good and bad points of each letter and put them in rank order.
- Write down your findings.
- Give your reasons for your final choice, matching those reasons to the job specifications. You should be able to justify your decision.
- Compare your results with others in the class. Were there any differences in the rank order?

TASK 9

Now write your own personal letter of application for the same placement. What differences are there between your letter and the one you ranked first?

Candidate 1

Dear Sir/Madam

I am a 16-year-old pupil currently studying ten GCSE subjects (including English and maths). I would like to be considered for the job because I feel that I possess the necessary qualifications and meet the requirements of your person specification.

In my last school report, my estimated grades in English and maths were As, and my teachers all commented on what a conscientious worker I am.

My retail experience is extensive. I have held down a job at my local supermarket for the past two years, and in this capacity have come into contact with a wide range of people and situations. There are four part-time staff working on Saturdays, and I have recently been given responsibility for working out lunch and tea-break duties. I believe that my confidence has grown in this time and that I work well as a member of a team.

I am on the editorial board of the school magazine, which is produced each term. Part of my responsibility has been to publicise the magazine both in and out of school and I have written adverts to promote the publication. I am aware of the pressures of working to deadlines and of writing for specific audiences.

I feel that with my background of working both in the retail trade and in the media, I am appropriately qualified to join your company. I have a good sense of humour and I am an enthusiastic worker.

I look forward to hearing from you in the near future.

Yours faithfully

Candidate 2

Dear Sir/Madam

At present, I am completing my GCSE course at school. I am studying not eight, not nine, but ten subjects including those most precious commodities Mathematics, English and English Literature. My estimated grades show that I am on course for A grades in all subjects. However, I feel my teachers are erring on the conservative side and I am certain to gain A* in the majority of my subjects.

In those all too rare moments when I am not studying the finer points of Literature or the great theories of Mathematics, I work in the local office of a national news communicator. Amongst the many intricate tasks I am trusted to perform, I operate the cash regulatory hardware when purchases are made. Also, on a daily basis, I brave the elements as a news delivery system operative. In this role I visit, and often meet, a large clientele who are most appreciative of my actions.

I should point out that my powers of persuasion are legendary. I have won the school debating cup three years in a row against some pretty powerful competition. I use this knowledge of persuasive techniques in another role — that of Editor of my local community newsletter, 'The Carsley Chronicle'. This monthly magazine contains a range of news, events and interviews with local celebrities. Since I took over as Editor, the circulation has risen from a simpering sixty to a staggering six hundred copies per month.

Finally, I should offer the following advice:

DON'T PASS UP THIS ONCE IN A LIFETIME OPPORTUNITY — CHOOSE ME NOW!

Yours faithfully

Candidate 3

Dear Sir or Madam,

I would like you to consider my application for the post of Junior Advertising Executive.

I am in the final year of my GCSE studies, and I am taking ten subjects in all. Throughout my school career I have worked hard and conscientiously and am therefore pleased to report that my estimated grades are all at A and above. Of particular relevance are my estimated grades in my three favourite subjects of English, English Literature and Mathematics, which are all at A* level. I intend to choose these three subjects, among others, to follow at A-Level next year.

My reasons for applying for the above placement are varied. I would eventually like to pursue a career in advertising and believe that the experience of working in a company such as yours would be invaluable. The opportunity to work collaboratively with a team of experts in the advertising field would be stimulating and would provide a challenge for my English skills.

I feel as though I possess the relevant retail and publishing experience your job specification requires. As part of my Business Studies coursework, I have set up and run a small publishing company which produced the last two highly successful editions of the school magazine. I managed to make a profit from the venture by encouraging local traders to pay for advertising within the magazine. The actual adverts I designed and wrote myself, and received several letters of thanks from the owners of shops whose sales were increased as a result.

With this background, I feel that I could be an asset to your company, and I look forward to working with you in the future.

Yours faithfully

Adapting text to the audience

Walk in to any travel agent and you will see hundreds of holiday brochures, advertising many locations and catering for different audiences. The primary purposes of a holiday brochure are to attract the attention of would-be tourists (holiday brochures are traditionally brightly coloured for this very reason) and then to persuade them that the holiday package advertised is the most suitable for them.

Look at the extracts from two different holiday brochures below (2wentys) and on the next page (Golden Years). Both advertise holidays in Tenerife, at the resort of Playa de las Americas, but they cater for very different audiences.

TASK 10

a) Compare the introductions to both holidays. How do these give clues as to the target audience?

b) Compare the two holidays using the following headings:
- emotive words
- language
- presentational features
- activities.

How do these give clues to the target audience? Write out a description of the target audience for each extract; include such things as age range and interests.

A

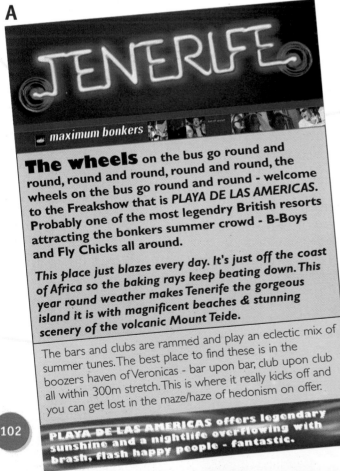

The wheels on the bus go round and round, round and round, round and round, the wheels on the bus go round and round - welcome to the Freakshow that is **PLAYA DE LAS AMERICAS.** Probably one of the most legendry British resorts attracting the bonkers summer crowd - B-Boys and Fly Chicks all around.

This place just blazes every day. It's just off the coast of Africa so the baking rays keep beating down. This year round weather makes Tenerife the gorgeous island it is with magnificent beaches & stunning scenery of the volcanic Mount Teide.

The bars and clubs are rammed and play an eclectic mix of summer tunes. The best place to find these is in the boozers haven of Veronicas - bar upon bar, club upon club all within 300m stretch. This is where it really kicks off and you can get lost in the maze/haze of hedonism on offer.

PLAYA DE LAS AMERICAS offers legendary sunshine and a nightlife overflowing with brash, flash happy people - fantastic.

maximum bonkers

Rebecca *apartments:*

PLAYA DE LAS AMERICAS

Exclusive to **2wentys**, the **Rebecca** Apartments lie deep in the heart of the resort, and form a complex with the adjacent Piramides Apartments. Guests at the Rebecca can use the many **facilities** at the Piramides - in addition to the swimming pool with sun terrace area, poolside bar, sunbeds, there is also a pool table and a supermarket (milk, tea bag, Ribena, Umbongo - **yummy**). The on-site restaurant serves both sna and set meals, including a full GREASY JOE breakfast.

At the Piramides next door, the guys put on some top notch **ents** to keep your holiday **bobbing** along.

Only 500m away, lined with a bustling array of bars and shopping arcades, is the dark sand of Playa de las Americas' volcanic beach with a selection of watersports available. For **evenings out** you ca beat the renowned Veronicas Centre, only a 5 minute stroll away, w its selection of restaurants, bars and clubs.

Prices shown are for Self catering based on 3 sharing a studio, 4 sharing a one bedroom or 6 sharing a two bedroom apartment. All have bath, shower, WC, kitchenette and balcony or terrace. Saf deposit boxes are available from reception (payable locally).

Tenerife is the largest of the Canary Islands – now well established as a favourite winter holiday destination. Lying just off the north west coast of Africa, the Canaries are blessed with a superb year round climate. Hence their other name: the 'Fortunate Islands'.

Tenerife has its own appeal, including the 12,000 foot Mount Teide which splits the islands into a lush and green northern side and a hotter and drier southern part.

Most of the Golden Years' hotels are on the northern side of Tenerife, in the cosmopolitan resort of Puerto de la Cruz, where the fabulous winter carnival takes place every February. The town has superb shopping facilities and an unbeatable location amidst the sub tropical splendours of the island. There are also Golden Years' hotels in the south of the island in very different resorts, Los Cristianos which is relaxing and another in Playa de las Americas, which is more bustling, on the southern coast.

Outstanding natural beauty is the only way to describe the profusion of bougainvillaeas and hibiscus, banana plantations and pine woods on the foothills of Mount Teide.

A trip to the top of Mount Teide will reward you with breathtaking views as you look out in one direction across the arid landscape of Las Canadas and northwards to the emerald green vegetation way below.

On another occasion, the mountain scenery at Pico del Ingles will enthrall you; and why not explore the Mercedes Forest, at the former capital of la Laguna.

You'll be equally impressed by the local wines and speciality fish dishes as well as the choice available at international restaurants situated throughout the island. Nature provides the sun and scenery whilst the locals lay on the souvenirs of lace, ceramics and leather and, as if that's not enough, they're very friendly too.

PLAYA DE LAS AMERICAS
HOTEL LAS DALIAS
A A A A

"Five minutes from the beach, bars and restaurants, this quality hotel makes a lovely base for a lively holiday."

Positioned in the San Eugenio area of Playa de las Americas, this fine hotel puts you just 500 metres from strolls on the sandy beach. About 300 metres further, in the busy Pueblo Canario Centre, you'll find a broad range of restaurants, bars and shops - so all the essential holiday ingredients are within easy reach of Las Dalias.

The hotel itself is as lively as the resort in which it stands - though the sunbathing terraces round the two pools can provide a leisurely spot. Sports enthusiasts may enjoy a challenging game on the squash and tennis courts, or a slightly less energetic session of pool or table tennis. Should more relaxing pastimes be your pleasure, there's a comfortable lounge bar, TV room and card room. Regular daytime activities include darts and quizzes, while dancing, live music and a weekly Canarian night are features of the evening entertainment programme. Meals are served buffet style in the hotel restaurant - so you can always choose your favourite foods from the very varied fayre.

The location of this property is unsuitable for people with walking difficulties/disabilities.

All rooms have safety deposit box, mini bar, air conditioning (all payable locally), satellite TV, telephone, bathroom and balcony.

OFFICIAL RATING: 4 star
SIZE: 429 rooms on 9 floors, 3 lifts

On the following pages are two pieces about the possibility of humans living on a planet other than Earth. The first is an article which predicts that soon there will be people living on the moon. The second gives some information about a company which is hoping to develop rockets which would be able to fly tourists into space, and eventually land on the moon or Mars. There are also some illustrations to show what conditions might be like there. Read both accounts carefully.

TASK 11

Imagine that the systems described in the second account have been successfully developed. You are working for the travel company in charge of flights to the moon or Mars. Your task is to put together a brochure which persuades people to fly to these new locations. Use information from the articles to help you, and make sure you adopt some of the persuasive techniques you have already studied in this unit.

The following headings might help you:
- cost • travel dates • expected journey times • accommodation
- excursions • activities • background information about the destination
- special offers.

You should choose a target audience before you begin to write.

PRIME REAL ESTATE ON THE MOON PICKED FOR FUTURE HUMAN COLONIES

By Robert Roy Britt

If you're trying to figure out where to put the first lunar subdivision, the same rules apply as on Earth: location, location, location. And what would you look for? A good exposure, of course, and perhaps a bit of water. But your goals are different: The sunlight is needed for power, and the water would sustain humans and provide fuel for rockets.

That in mind, a group of researchers has identified three locations near the Moon's south pole that would be the best spots for any future lunar colony. Each spot gets loads of sunlight and sits next to an area that is believed to harbour large stores of frozen water.

THE ULTIMATE GOAL: A MOON BASE

A future base on the Moon, at least initially, would not likely resemble most earthbound communities. A lunar colony would be a specific outpost and launch pad.

According to a NASA paper on the Lunar Prospector mission, which contributed to the discovery of water, 'The moon may well be the site of the first extraterrestrial human outpost in the solar system – a feat which would permit ongoing lunar and astronomy studies, long-range observation of the Earth as well as serving as a platform from which to explore the rest of the solar system.'

The uses for ice and the oxygen and hydrogen that could be extracted from it range from the critical to the more imaginative. From supporting human life to providing rocket fuel, the ice could facilitate trips to Mars and, as NASA puts it, create 'the ability to refuel rockets at a lunar 'filling station' and making transport to and from the Moon more economical by at least a factor of ten.'

'With water there you could have enclosed areas to grow plants, grow your own food, make your own fuel, make your own air,' says Anthony Cook of the Griffith Observatory. 'You don't have to launch all that stuff from big rockets. Or the Earth.'

THE KEY TO A MOON BASE: WATER AND SUNLIGHT

In March of 1998, NASA announced the discovery of strong evidence of water ice around both poles of the Moon, saying there could be enough to support a colony of 2,000 for a hundred years. The water, believed to be buried under 18 inches of lunar soil, may have come from comet impacts, NASA scientists say.

Sunlight would be another key, creating a more workable climate with a near-constant temperature. Though still well below freezing, the more even climate would be easier to work in, the researchers said. In contrast, areas along the Moon's equator are exposed to direct sunlight for long periods but are plunged into equally long stretches of darkness, when temperatures plummet.

SP/CE™
adventures

submit your info &
join our mailing list

Steps To Space™

The fourth of our Steps to Space
Where reality exceeds your dreams ...

Space Adventures is proud to offer you the opportunity to personally experience the grandeur of space.

In 1961, Alan Shepard was launched on a 15 minute sub-orbital flight that made history, as he became the first American in space. Today, Space Adventures is working with the leading space vehicle development companies to bring you this same, once-in-a-lifetime opportunity. We are now taking advanced reservations for flights aboard these new vehicles.

These flights are preceded by an astronaut-developed, 6-day training program during which attendees learn all about the vehicle and spaceflight. They will come to understand the basic science of space travel: from propulsion to guidance; from communications to recovery.

When the much anticipated launch day arrives, attendees will don flight suits and board the vehicle which will return them astronauts. Depending on the launch vehicle they choose, they will either blast off from the ground with the roar of rockets or depart from an airport with a jet assisted take-off. The flight to 100 kilometres (62 miles) altitude will be breathtaking, the experience of a lifetime!

The entire ride will last between 30 to 90 minutes, depending on the vehicle chosen. Having taken the same challenge as Alan Shepard, they will have earned their astronaut wings.

Spacer Cruiser® – Designed for Space Tourism

When Vela Technology Development began the creation of the Space Cruiser, they took the view that passengers are more than just another kind of payload. The result is a vehicle that has been designed from the inside out to maximise the space experience. The spaceplane provides first-class accommodation for six passengers and two crew in a large cabin over eight feet in diameter, with passenger seats that fold into the floor to present the largest volume for weightless activity. Large windows provide a spectacular view of the Earth from space. The acceleration during boost is controlled to be no more than two gees to maintain a comfortable ride and make health requirements less stringent for passengers, because this time everyone gets to go!

Passenger safety is the prime requirement for space tourism. To provide the lowest-risk ride possible, the Space Cruiser uses no unproven technology. Even the method of air launch from a carrier vehicle has been used on almost two hundred flights of the X-15, and hundreds of other X-plane flights since 1947. Pressure-fed rocket engines have a legacy dating back to Robert Goddard's first rocket in 1926. The pressure-fed engines of the Space Cruiser burn nitrous oxide and propane, which are room temperature storable and produce no harmful exhaust products. The jet engines and avionics come from the same methods used in the construction of business jets.

The flight experience for the space tourist begins with the Space Cruiser attached to the underside of the Sky Lifter® carrier vehicle. The Sky Lifter takes off from a conventional airfield and carries the Space Cruiser to over 40,000 feet, where the spaceplane is released. The Space Cruiser's rocket engines are ignited, and the vehicle accelerates to over 2,000 mph. When the engines stop, the seats fold into the floor and passengers will experience over two and a half minutes of free fall as the Space Cruiser climbs to over 100 km (62 miles). As the Space Cruiser begins to descend the seats return to the upright position and the rocket engines are fired briefly to slow the descent before reentry.

After the Space Cruiser reenters the atmosphere the jet engines are started, and the vehicle returns to the airfield just like a business jet.

Speaking to persuade

On occasions, you may be asked to prepare a speech in which you attempt to persuade an audience to a particular point of view. You should approach such a task in the same way as you would any persuasive written assignment – many of the skills and techniques can be used in your speech and you should aim to include an appropriate range.

Study the speech below, which is by the former President of South Africa, Nelson Mandela. He gave this speech to an audience of world leaders when he was appointed President in 1994. It is a very powerful speech, even though he is not specifically persuading his audience to do or think anything.

TASK 12

a) How many persuasive devices can you detect in the speech?

b) What message does Nelson Mandela give in his speech? For example, what is he trying to get the world leaders to think or do? Look in particular at the language, structure and style.

c) With a partner, discuss how you think the speech should be read and then practise reading the speech out loud. Think about:
- which words you need to emphasise
- where you need to pause for dramatic effect
- the tone of the speech.

Your Majesties,
Your Highnesses,
Distinguished Guests,
Comrades and Friends,

Today, all of us do, by our presence here, and by our celebration in other parts of our country and the world, confer glory and hope to newborn liberty.

Out of the experience of an extraordinary human disaster that lasted too long, must be born a society of which all humanity will be proud.

Our daily deeds as ordinary South Africans must produce an actual South African reality that will reinforce humanity's belief in justice, strengthen its confidence in the nobility of the human soul and sustain all our hopes for a glorious life for all.

All this we owe both to ourselves and to the people of the world who are so well represented here today.

To my compatriots, I have no hesitation in saying that each one of us is as intimately attached to the soil of this beautiful country as are the famous jacaranda trees of Pretoria and the mimosa trees of the bushveld.

Each time one of us touches the soil of this land, we feel a sense of personal renewal. The national mood changes as the seasons change.

We are moved by a sense of joy and exhilaration when the grass turns green and the flowers bloom.

That spiritual and physical oneness we all share with this common homeland explains the depth of the pain we all carried in our hearts as we saw our country tear itself apart in a terrible conflict, and as we saw it spurned, outlawed and isolated by the peoples of the world precisely because it has become the universal base of the pernicious ideology and practice of racism and racial oppression.

We, the people of South Africa, feel fulfilled that humanity has taken us back into its bosom, that we, who were outlaws not so long ago, have today been given the rare privilege to be host to the nations of the world on our own soil.

We thank all our distinguished international guests for having come to take possession with the people of our country of what is, after all, a common victory for justice, for peace, for human dignity.

We trust that you will continue to stand by us as we tackle the challenges of building peace, prosperity, non-sexism, non-racism and democracy.

We deeply appreciate the role that the masses of our people and their political mass democratic, religious, women, youth, business, traditional and other leaders have played to bring about this conclusion. Not least among them is my Second Deputy President, the Honourable F. W. de Klerk.

We would also like to pay tribute to our security forces, in all their ranks, for the distinguished role they have played in securing our first democratic election and the transition to democracy, from blood-thirsty forces which still refuse to see the light.

The time for the healing of the wounds has come.

The moment to bridge the chasms that divide us has come.

The time to build is upon us.

We have, at last achieved our political emancipation. We pledge ourselves to liberate all our people from the continuing bondage of poverty, deprivation, suffering, gender and other discrimination.

We succeeded to take our last steps to freedom in conditions of relative peace. We commit ourselves to the construction of a complete, just and lasting peace.

We have triumphed in the effort to implant hope in the breasts of the millions of our people. We enter into a covenant that we shall build the society in which all South Africans, both black and white, will be able to walk tall, without any fear in their hearts, assured of their inalienable right to human dignity – a rainbow nation at peace with itself and the world.

As a token of its commitment to the renewal of our country, the new Interim Government of National Unity will, as a matter of urgency, address the issue of amnesty for various categories of our people who are currently serving terms of imprisonment.

We dedicate this day to all the heros and heroines in this country and the rest of the world who sacrificed in many ways and surrendered their lives so that we could be free.

Their dreams have become reality. Freedom is their reward.

We are both humbled and elevated by the honour and privilege that you, the people of South Africa, have bestowed on us, as the first president of a united, democratic, non-racial and non-sexist government.

We understand it still that there is no easy road to freedom.

We know it well that none of us acting alone can achieve success.

We must therefore act together as a united people, for national reconciliation, for nation building, for the birth of a new world.

Let there be justice for all.

Let there be peace for all.

Let there be work, bread, water and salt for all.

Let each know that for each the body, the mind and the soul have been freed to fulfil themselves.

Never, never and never again shall it be that this beautiful land will again experience the oppression of one by another and suffer the indignity of being the skunk of the world.

Let freedom reign.

The sun shall never set on so glorious a human achievement!

God bless Africa!

TASK 13

Write a speech to be given to a class or Year assembly on a topic you feel strongly about. Make your speech as persuasive as possible by using the techniques you have studied in this unit. You could choose a topic yourself or pick one from this list:

- Why vegetarian food is a healthier option
- Smoking should be banned from all public places
- Prison life today is too comfortable
- Blood sports have no place in 20th-century Britain.

Assessment – smoking

Printed below is the opening paragraph from a pupil's response to Task 13. Read it carefully, and take note of the comments that the examiner made.

Strengths

Involves the audience.

Addresses the task right at the start.

Presents a point of view – appropriate in a persuasive assignment. Attempts to give reasons why.

Opening A

I think that smoking should be banned from all public places because its not fair that we should breathe in filthy dirty smoke that comes straight from someones lungs. Its disgusting when you walk into a room where somebodies been smoking and its terrible you know straight away that they've been smoking because of the smell. It gets in your hair and onto your clothes and you have to go straight home and have a bath to get rid of the smell. People can get cancer just from breathing in someone elses smoke even when they try not to because people who smoke are just being selfish they don't think of what they are doing to others.

Weaknesses

Begins to give reasons too early – this is best left until later as this is an introductory paragraph.

New sentence needed here.

Not necessary – already used 'disgusting' to express opinion.

General comments on A

A fairly lively opening paragraph which does try to involve the audience. However, the points are introduced too early and really need to be developed in much greater detail. There are also some punctuation and grammar errors.

TASK 14

As you can see, the examiner has placed comments at appropriate places on the page. What kind of grade do you think this would have achieved in an exam? How could the opening have been improved?

Now look carefully at opening B. Write down the strengths and weaknesses of this as an opening. Remember this is supposed to be a persuasive speech so you must assess it on how well it is written for this purpose, not on whether you agree with the content.

When you have finished this task, discuss your findings with a neighbour and then complete the speech in your own words.

Opening B

Good morning.

Today, I am going to talk to you about a subject I am sure we all feel strongly about but will probably not all agree on – whether smoking should be banned from all public places. Already, I can see from your faces whether you agree or disagree with this statement and this is probably related to whether or not you are a smoker. Whatever point of view you hold at the moment, I intend to convince you by the end of my speech that smoking should be banned from all public places. I have collected together a wide range of information, facts and opinions from a wide range of sources, and I am sure that by the end of my presentation, even the most hardened smoker will be convinced that smoking is expensive, unhealthy and anti-social, and that it should be banned from all public places immediately.

Unit 6 Argument

Understanding the term 'argument'

When you consider what is meant by the word 'argument', the first thing you probably think of is the everyday sense that is attached to the word – two people having a heated conversation, perhaps quarrelling with each other.

However, in this section, you will be thinking of the word 'argument' in a different way. The *Collins New School Dictionary* gives the following definition of the word:

A point or set of reasons you use to try to convince people about something.

That sounds a little like persuasive writing, doesn't it? For instance, when a holiday company produces a brochure, are they not trying to provide the reader with a set of reasons to persuade them to go to a particular place?

They certainly are trying to persuade the reader, but they are doing so in a different way. Rather than producing a set of reasons, they are using *emotive* and *descriptive language* to do the persuading.

TASK 1

Pick out language used emotively and/or descriptively in the article below. It is taken from a brochure advertising holidays in Canada.

Your holiday is a celebration of Canada's scenic splendour, fascinating past, and dynamic present. Commencing in the cosmopolitan city of Toronto, traverse the popular Muskoka region en route to the wilds of Algonquin Provincial Park. Tour Ottawa, Canada's political heart, before crossing into Quebec.

The rugged landscape of the Laurentian Mountains provides a taste of Quebec's pristine beauty. From the resort of Mont-Tremblant, embark on a tour of the urban gems of Quebec City and vibrant Montreal (pictured) ...

In contrast, the article below provides a good example of argumentative writing. Here, the author of the article is certainly trying to convince people about something – in this case, the seriousness of the bullying problem in schools. However, the author tries to support their view by presenting *evidence* which demonstrates the nature, frequency and severity of the bullying problem, rather than by the use of descriptive or emotive language.

Read the article below, and then answer the questions which follow.

BULLYING – Time for Action

According to the charity Kids, in the last six months, there have been eight recorded cases of young girls taking overdoses to escape from bullies. Some might say that as a national figure this is very low, but I would argue that even one case is too many, and that the issue of bullying in all its forms needs to be discussed at a national level.

It is often assumed that bullying is essentially something that is done by boys, and that most victims of bullying are also boys. Certainly, figures suggest that the great majority of bullies are boys, with over 80 per cent of school exclusions for bullying being handed out to boys. However, Jane Mitchell, Director of Kids, suggests in her paper, *Bullying – The Real Truth*, that the official figures actually mask the truth, for schools tend to exclude pupils only for physical bullying, whereas other forms of bullying are equally damaging, although little is done about it.

Mitchell believes that perhaps as much as 40 per cent of bullying is actually done by girls, but that the forms of bullying are rather different and, often, not brought to the attention of staff in schools. *Bullying – The Real Truth* puts forward the view that girls are more likely to be articulate in their bullying strategies – they go in for name-calling, or sending girls to Coventry. While this would seem to be rather mild – everybody knows the old adage, 'Sticks and stones may break my bones but words will never harm me' – the truth is that words *do* harm, and sometimes cause very serious long-term damage

to the victims. For instance, such bullying led to Ms Mitchell having to deal with a 13-year-old girl who had tried to kill herself after being bullied by a gang of girls. Every day, they had chased her home from school, shouting insults and threats. She did not report it to the school or her mother, but took an overdose of her mother's sleeping pills and was fortunate to be saved after being found, comatose, in her bedroom.

Such stories do starkly bring home the bullying problem, but the official figures of Childline paint an equally disturbing picture of the severity of the bullying problem today.

Childline was launched in 1988, providing a listening ear for children who were victims of bullying and abuse, either at school or at home. In the first two years, over 2,000 children had rung for counselling, and of these, less that 200 had, at the time, told either their parents or their school.

While schools have made great steps since 1988 to try to ensure that bullying issues are reported and dealt with, it is still difficult to know how much of the 'bullying iceberg' can be seen, even today. The old code of honour – that children must not tell their teachers or their parents – is still around, if a little eroded, and victims of bullies still often feel that it is they who are weak and somehow at fault, and not the bullies.

Perhaps most worrying, though, is that bullies tend to go on to violent crime, for research shows that over 90 per cent of those convicted for violent offences also exhibited violent or anti-social behaviour when at school. Surely, if we can open up a national debate now, leading to nationally focused action, then there is just a chance that fewer of today's young bullies will become tomorrow's criminals. ●

WS 38

TASK 2

a) What *evidence* does the author of the article put forward to contradict arguments that most bullying is done by boys?

b) What *evidence* does the author put forward to suggest that name-calling is just as harmful as physical bullying?

c) What *evidence* suggests that reported bullying only represents 'the tip of the iceberg'?

d) What *evidence* does the author put forward to support their view that a national debate, followed by national action, is needed?

Analysing an argument

Having established the basic difference between persuasive writing and argumentative writing, it is now time to look at how argumentative writing is structured.

Typically, a paragraph of argumentative writing will be introduced by a **main idea**; this is the *general point* that the author wishes to make.

Then, they will support this view by evidence – this consists of **supporting details**. Evidence can be presented in the form of *facts* or *statistics*, but equally, it can be *anecdotal evidence* (which means stories about people's own experiences).

If you look back to the previous article, you will see how the author does this:

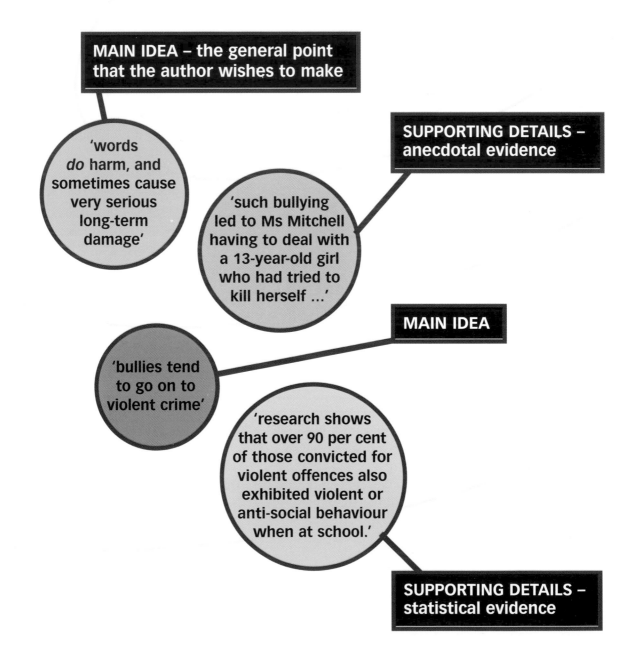

MAIN IDEA – the general point that the author wishes to make

'words *do* harm, and sometimes cause very serious long-term damage'

SUPPORTING DETAILS – anecdotal evidence

'such bullying led to Ms Mitchell having to deal with a 13-year-old girl who had tried to kill herself …'

MAIN IDEA

'bullies tend to go on to violent crime'

'research shows that over 90 per cent of those convicted for violent offences also exhibited violent or anti-social behaviour when at school.'

SUPPORTING DETAILS – statistical evidence

In these examples, only one supporting detail is given to support each main idea. However, quite often a writer will support a main idea with two, three or more supporting details.

TASK 3

Look at the example below. Decide what is the main idea, and then which details support that main idea. (Paragraphs have deliberately been omitted from this passage.) Set out your response in the form of a diagram, as outlined below.

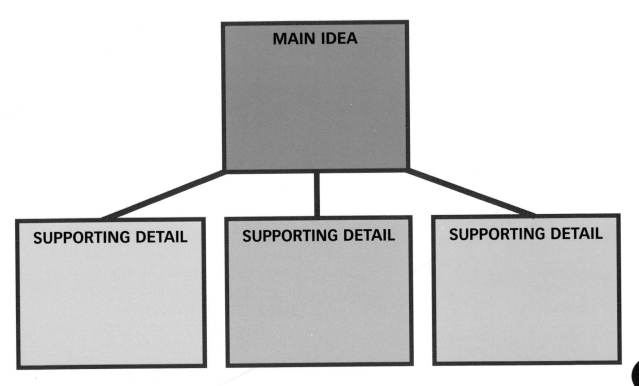

We are living in a violent society, and our schools are no longer 'safe havens' from danger. Consider the case of 13-year-old Rebecca Smith, who committed suicide rather than face another day of the repeated taunts about her size; and James Adams, who was brutally teased merely because he was 'clever'; or remember Jane Mann, the 23-year-old who gave up her job as a French teacher because she could no longer put up with the 'yobbishness' of the youths she was trying, in vain, to educate.

MAIN IDEA

SUPPORTING DETAIL

SUPPORTING DETAIL

SUPPORTING DETAIL

WS
39

TASK 4

Now complete the same exercise for the passage below. You have to decide how many main ideas there are in this piece of writing, and how many supporting details for each main idea. (Once more, paragraphs have been omitted from the passage.) Try to summarise all the information in your own words as far as possible.

It is sometimes suggested that there is a 'blueprint' for a bully, and to some extent, this is true. Research has shown that most bullies come from dysfunctional home environments. That is where they pick up their anti-social habits. George Jones, a 16-year-old, self-confessed bully, was, for instance, frequently hit by his father. On two occasions, indeed, he was admitted to hospital with arm fractures from blows administered by his father. On the other hand, Theresa Jones, aged 14, who was expelled from a London school following a series of bullying incidents, revealed that although she was not herself subjected to any physical violence, her home was a place of constant argument and bickering. Interestingly, over 75% of bullies are said to come from homes where relationships are less than affectionate. If there is a 'blueprint' for a bully, is there also a 'blueprint' for the victim of bullying? Briefly, the answer is no. Parents of victims sometimes go to great extremes to try to help their children, because they mistakenly believe that the fault lies with their children – Sheila Wilson, mother of 12-year-old Tracey, helped her to lose weight because of the name–calling that she was suffering. Tracey did lose nearly two stone, but the bullies, far from being quietened, recognised the effect they were having on their victim, and though the 'flavour' of the name–calling altered, the jibes only intensified. Therefore, while it is often said that victims of bullying are people who are 'different' – they wear unfashionable clothes, or they are too fat, or too thin, or have a different skin colour, or their ears stick out, etc. – in reality, research demonstrates that these are mere 'excuses' that have been given for bullying behaviour; in fact there is very little commonality among the victims of bullying. So what should a parent do if she finds that her child is a victim of bullying? Firstly, she should contact the school, and talk with her child's form tutor. She should find out what the school is doing to tackle bullying. Also, it would be a good idea to try to talk to the bully's parents, to ascertain whether he/she has any history of bullying behaviour. Perhaps most importantly, she should demand to know what action is going to be taken to deal with the bully to prevent him/her from bullying in the future.

TASK 5

When you have completed Task 4, consider what you have learned about the way in which argumentative texts are structured. Write a statement of no more than fifty words, summarising what you have learned so far.

WS
40

TASK 6

a) Read through the passage on the opposite page again, and decide where you would put paragraphs in the text. Indicate the position of each new paragraph by quoting its first three or four words, and then briefly explain why a new paragraph is required at that point. For example:

> 'It is sometimes suggested...'
> Here, the author is introducing the idea that there is a blueprint for a bully.

b) Next, read through the additional sentences printed below. Show where you would add them to the text, by quoting the three or four words that would come immediately before the additional text. Briefly explain the reasons for your decision.

The first one has been done for you as an example.

A Similarly 10-year-old Joanne convinced her father to pay for cosmetic surgery to correct a minor 'bump' in her nose, because she thought it would put an end to the spiteful comments that she had been subjected to.

B 50% of bullies indicate that they come from families where relationships often 'break down completely'.

C If it is true that a bullying 'blueprint' exists, this largely being caused by poor parenting skills, then schools can play a major role in helping parents to adopt more effective parenting skills, and thus break the cycle that leads to the problem of bullying.

D If this is the first known occasion, action now might 'nip it in the bud'.

E Briefly, *anybody* can be the victim of bullying, and *anything* can be its subject.

Example

> A) '... the jibes only intensified'. The author has just given one example of how parents try to 'change' their children to help them avoid bullying. This is a second example.

Writing an argumentative essay

In the first section of this unit, you learned that, paragraph by paragraph, argumentative writing often follows this structure:

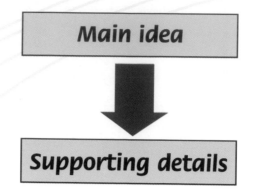

The main idea is the main point that you wish to make.

The supporting details can take the form of:

- anecdotal evidence – stories from your own or others' personal experience
- factual/statistical evidence – information gathered from books, newspapers, magazines, the Internet, etc.

Let us consider this question:

Is there really a drugs problem today, or is it merely an invention of the media?

When you are writing an argumentative essay, the first thing you need to do is **form a view** about the question. This should not simply be something off the top of your head, but should be an opinion formed after looking at the *evidence*, and perhaps drawing from your own *personal experience* or that of people you know.

When you have formed your opinion, then you are ready to write an introductory paragraph. You should:

- express your view clearly, so that the reader knows the *direction* that your essay will take
- ensure that you grab the reader's *attention*; for instance, you might make a forthright statement, or begin with a startling or surprising piece of information.

TASK 7

Skim read the information on drugs which has been printed over the next three pages. When you have done so, read the four 'openings' to arguments on page 120.

Which openings do you think are successful in achieving the criteria above?
Give reasons for your choices.

Drug and Alcohol Abuse – Some Statistics

Drugs

In 1996, an estimated 13.0 million Americans were current illicit drug users, meaning they had used an illicit drug in the month prior to interview. This represents no change from 1995 when the estimate was 12.8 million. The number of current illicit drug users was at its highest level in 1979 when there were 25 million.

Following a significant increase from 1992 to 1995, between 1995 and 1996 there was a decrease in the rate of past month illicit drug use among youths aged 12–17. The rate was 5.3 per cent in 1992, 10.9 per cent in 1995, and 9.0 per cent in 1996. The decrease between 1995 and 1996 occurred in the younger part of this age group, i.e., those aged 12 to 15 years.

For those aged 18–25 years, the rate of past month illicit drug use increased from 13.3 per cent in 1994 to 15.6 per cent in 1996. The rate of past month cocaine use also increased in this age group during this period, from 1.2 per cent to 2.0 per cent.

There were an estimated 2.4 million people who started using marijuana in 1995. This was about the same number as in 1994. The annual number of marijuana initiates rose between 1991 and 1994.

The overall number of current cocaine users did not change significantly between 1995 and 1996 (1.45 million in 1995 and 1.75 million in 1996). This is down from a peak of 5.7 million in 1985.

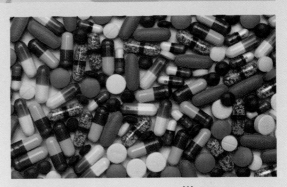

Nevertheless, there were still an estimated 652,000 Americans who used cocaine for the first time in 1995.

There were an estimated 141,000 new heroin users in 1995, and there has been an increasing trend in new heroin use since 1992. A large proportion of these recent new users were smoking, snorting, or sniffing heroin, and most were under age 26. The estimated number of past month users increased from 68,000 in 1993 to 216,000 in 1996.

Alcohol

In 1996, 109 million Americans aged 12 and older had used alcohol in the past month (51 per cent of the population). About 32 million engaged in binge drinking (five or more drinks on at least one occasion in the past month) and about 11 million were heavy drinkers (drinking five or more drinks per occasion on 5 or more days in the past 30 days).

About 9 million current drinkers were aged 12–20 in 1996. Of these, 4.4 million were binge drinkers, including 1.9 million heavy drinkers.

Nearly half of all Americans over the age of 12 are consumers of alcohol. Although most drink only occasionally or moderately, there are an estimated 10 to 15 million alcoholics or problem drinkers in the United States, with more than 100,000 deaths each year attributed to alcohol. Among the nation's alcoholics and problem drinkers are as many as 4.5 million adolescents, and adolescents are disproportionately involved in alcohol-related automobile accidents, the leading cause of death among Americans 15 to 24 years old.

Health hazards

Neurological dangers include impaired motor co-ordination, memory defects, hallucinations, blackouts, and seizures.

Cardiological problems include elevated blood pressure and heart rate, risk of stroke and heart failure.

Liver disease caused by chronic alcohol abuse, including alcoholic fatty liver, hepatitis, and cirrhosis, kills 25,000 Americans each year.

Cocaine and Crack

The proportion of high school seniors who have used cocaine at least once in their lifetimes has increased from a low of 5.9 per cent in 1994 to 9.8 per cent in 1999. However, this is lower than its peak of 17.3 per cent in 1985. Current (past month) use of cocaine by seniors decreased from a high of 6.7 per cent in 1985 to 2.6 per cent in 1999. Also in 1999, 7.7 per cent of 10th-graders had tried cocaine at least once, up from a low of 3.3 per cent in 1992. The percentage of 8th-graders who had ever tried cocaine has increased from a low of 2.3 per cent in 1991 to 4.7 per cent in 1999.

Health hazards

Some users of cocaine report feelings of restlessness, irritability, and anxiety. An appreciable tolerance to the high may be developed, and many addicts report that they seek but fail to achieve as much pleasure as they did from their first exposure. In rare instances, sudden death can occur on the first use of cocaine or unexpectedly thereafter. However, there is no way to determine who is prone to sudden death.

High doses of cocaine and/or prolonged use can trigger paranoia.

Smoking crack cocaine can produce a particularly aggressive paranoid behavior in users.

When addicted individuals stop using cocaine, they often become depressed. This also may lead to further cocaine use to alleviate depression.

Prolonged cocaine snorting can result in ulceration of the mucous membrane of the nose and can damage the nasal septum enough to cause it to collapse.

Cocaine-related deaths are often a result of cardiac arrest or seizures followed by respiratory arrest.

Heroin

Heroin is a highly addictive drug, and its use is a serious problem in America. Current estimates suggest that nearly 600,000 people need treatment for heroin addiction. Recent studies suggest a shift from injecting heroin to snorting or smoking because of increased purity and the misconception that these forms of use will not lead to addiction.

Reports from the Drug Abuse Warning Network (DAWN), which collects data on drug-related hospital emergency room episodes and drug-related deaths from 21 metropolitan areas, rank heroin second as the most frequently mentioned drug in overall drug-related deaths. From 1990 through 1995, the number of heroin-related episodes doubled. Between 1994 and 1995, there was a 19 per cent increase in heroin-related emergency department cases.

Health hazards

Heroin abuse is associated with serious health conditions, including fatal overdose, spontaneous abortion, collapsed veins, and infectious diseases, including HIV/AIDS and hepatitis.

Following initial euphoria, the user goes "on the nod," an alternately wakeful and drowsy state. Mental functioning becomes clouded due to the depression of the central nervous system.

Long-term effects of heroin appear after repeated use for some period of time. Chronic users may develop collapsed veins, infection of the heart lining and valves, abscesses, cellulitis, and liver disease. Pulmonary complications, including various types of pneumonia, may result from the poor health condition of the abuser, as well as from heroin's depressing effects on respiration.

Cannabis

After decreasing for over a decade, cannabis use among students began to increase in the early 1990s. From 1998 to 1999, use of cannabis at least once (lifetime use) increased among 12th- and 10th-graders, continuing the trend seen in recent years. The seniors' rate of lifetime use is higher than in any year since 1987, but all rates remain well below those seen in the late 1970s and early 1980s. Past year and past month cannabis use did not change significantly from 1998 to 1999 in any of the three grades, suggesting the sharp increase of recent years may be slowing.

Health hazards

There is as much exposure to cancer-causing chemicals from smoking one cannabis joint as smoking five tobacco cigarettes. And there is evidence that cannabis may limit the ability of the immune system to fight infection and disease.

Another concern is the drug's role as a "gateway drug," which makes subsequent use of more potent and disabling substances more likely. The Center on Addiction and Substance Abuse at Columbia University found adolescents who smoke cannabis 85 times more likely to use cocaine than their non-smoking peers. And 60 per cent of youngsters who use cannabis before they turn 15 later go on to use cocaine.

Openings

W S
41

TASK 8

Below are four openings to essays written in response to the question:

Is there really a drugs problem today, or is it merely an invention of the media?

For each opening, say whether you think:

- the writer has expressed their view clearly
- the writer has succeeded in grabbing the reader's attention.

1

In some ways, I think there is a drugs problem, but in other ways, I don't think there is. There are lots of people in America on drugs. I think they should all be put in prison. That would teach them a lesson.

2

Last weekend, in a night club in our town, an 18-year-old girl died after taking Ecstasy. She is certainly not the first person to die from this drug; she is not even the first this month. Unfortunately, she will not be the last.

This clearly shows that there is a genuine drugs problem in society today. Even one death is too much.

3

In a 1993 survey in the USA it was estimated that 68,000 people used heroin. In 1996 this figure had more than trebled, to 216,000.

Furthermore, between 1990 and 1995, the number of 'emergency room episodes' caused by heroin doubled.

How can anybody suggest, therefore, that there is not a real drugs problem today?

4

While society's drugs problem cannot be described as mere 'invention', the media does tend to exaggerate the seriousness of the problem.

It is interesting to note that in 1979 there were 25 million illicit drug users in the USA, yet by 1996 this figure had shrunk to only 15 million.

Developing the argument

So, having seen how you might begin this essay, and what constitutes a 'good' opening for such writing, you now have to consider how you might develop that writing.

TASK 9

a) Read the information on pages 117–19 more carefully. Then, write your own introductory paragraph to the question:

Is there really a drugs problem today, or is it merely an invention of the media?

Remember, you need to:
- express your view clearly
- grab your reader's attention.

b) Plan how you will develop your argument. Use the plan on page 113 to help you to do this.

c) There is a lot of information on pages 117–19 to provide you with some of the statistical evidence which you will certainly need for your supporting details. However, you might also wish to find out more information for yourself.

Think about consulting one or more of the following sources of information:
- school library
- local library
- magazines
- newspapers
- the Internet.

Remember, the more evidence that you have to support the views that you put forward, the more effective will be your essay.

TASK 10

When you have planned your essay, and are satisfied with its overall structure, draft it out in full.

A few tips

Tone and language

When you write your essay, remember that your writing should be formal. In particular, you should avoid colloquial (everyday) language, especially slang.

For example, this would be inappropriate:

Alcohol makes you stagger about, and it would be stupid to ride a bike after drinking. You also get a massive hangover if you drink too much.

Instead, it might be written as:

Alcohol can make people unable to balance or to judge distances, and it would therefore be unwise, for instance, to ride a bicycle after taking alcohol. A person who drinks excessively might also suffer from a headache and sickness on the following day.

Notice that the language in the second example is rather different:

stagger about ⟶ *unable to balance or to judge distances*

stupid ⟶ *unwise*

massive hangover ⟶ *suffer from a headache and sickness*

Notice also that the use of the second person (you) has been dropped: that form of expression is rather informal, and unsuitable when putting forward a serious argument.

So:

Alcohol makes ⟶ *can make **people** unable to balance*
you stagger about

***You** also get a* ⟶ *A **person** who drinks excessively*
massive hangover

Use of connectives

Connectives are very useful because they help you to shape your writing. Sometimes connectives are used at the beginning of a sentence, and sometimes they are used to join two sentences together.

Look at the ways connectives have been used in the examples below.

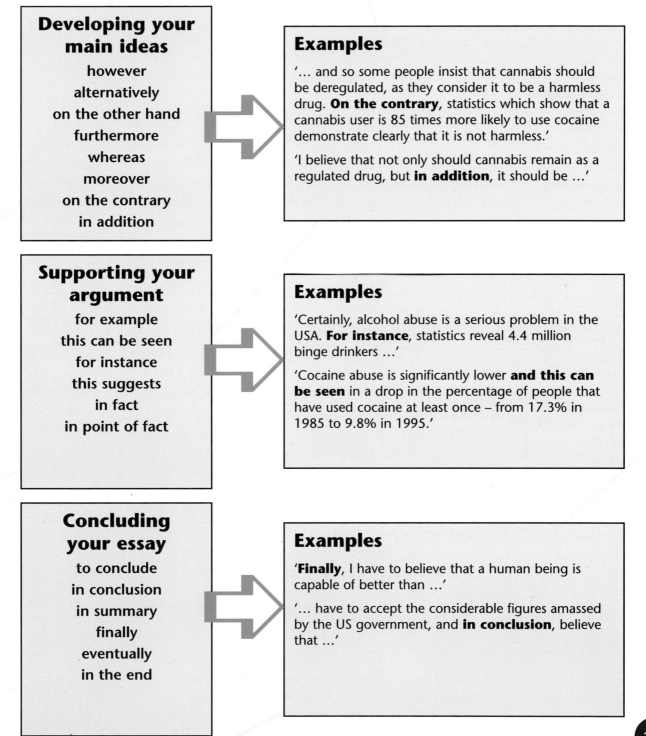

Developing your main ideas

however

alternatively

on the other hand

furthermore

whereas

moreover

on the contrary

in addition

Examples

'… and so some people insist that cannabis should be deregulated, as they consider it to be a harmless drug. **On the contrary**, statistics which show that a cannabis user is 85 times more likely to use cocaine demonstrate clearly that it is not harmless.'

'I believe that not only should cannabis remain as a regulated drug, but **in addition**, it should be …'

Supporting your argument

for example

this can be seen

for instance

this suggests

in fact

in point of fact

Examples

'Certainly, alcohol abuse is a serious problem in the USA. **For instance**, statistics reveal 4.4 million binge drinkers …'

'Cocaine abuse is significantly lower **and this can be seen** in a drop in the percentage of people that have used cocaine at least once – from 17.3% in 1985 to 9.8% in 1995.'

Concluding your essay

to conclude

in conclusion

in summary

finally

eventually

in the end

Examples

'**Finally**, I have to believe that a human being is capable of better than …'

'… have to accept the considerable figures amassed by the US government, and **in conclusion**, believe that …'

Assessment – argumentative writing

Printed below is a student's attempt at answering the question:

Some people believe that the cane should be reintroduced to British schools. Do you think that it should?

It has been marked by a GCSE examiner. Read it through, and take note of the comments that the examiner has made.

Reasonable opening – clearly shows the direction the essay will take.

Merely the plural of 'teacher' – no need for an apostrophe.

Needs a comma.

Good use of a 'signpost connective' – in this case, introducing a contrasting view.

Good use of connective to open the sentence. Again, good use of the rhetorical question.

> I don't think the cane should be reintroduced to British schools.
>
> This is because I think that schools and teacher's should set an example to pupils. How can schools tell pupils not to be violent, if they are hitting them with sticks at the same time? If schools are going to set a good example then they should teach pupils how to solve problems through talking instead of violence.
>
> On the other hand, my dad thinks that schools were better when they had the cane. He says that classes were better behaved then how does he know? In fact, although he goes to parents' evening, he hasn't actually been in a classroom for twenty years, so how does he know how pupils behave today? Almost all classes in my school are very well behaved, and nobody has to be threaten by the cane. We learn because we understand how important it is to learn today. Anyway, in the next breath dad tells me what things they used to get up to, so I'm not sure people really were better behaved then.

This is good. The use of the word 'sticks' reminds the rea[d] of the brutality of the cane. Good use of a rhetorical question [a question that do[es] not really require an answer[.]

Main idea.

This needs a full stop, especially as the first part is a statement and the second part is a question.

Good use of anecdotal detail to support more argument.

Past tense – add 'ed'.

The tone of this section is completely wrong. This is written in a colloquial, informal style, as can be seen in the word 'anyway', which opens the sentence, and in the slang term 'in the next breath': the tone of an argumentative essay should be formal.

Repetitive — repeating the idea outlined in the second paragraph.

Useful combination of connectives.

Again, as the student begins this sentence with 'As I have said', it suggests that their writing needs to be better organised.

> I think that one of the most important points is that if teachers beat pupils when they do not behave, they are actually teaching them that people can be contraled by violence.
>
> However, in the end the question is one that does not really need to be asked there is a European Court of human rights and no child in Europe can be beaten in school. In point of fact, even if Britain was to think that this would be a good idea, the court would not allow Britain to take such a decision.
>
> As I have said, most pupils in our school behave very well. However, if they do not behave, then pupils can be given extra work, or a detention, or there parents can be sent for. In extreme cases, pupils can be suspended so I think there's enough.
>
> In the end, I cannot see that the reintroduction of the cane would serve any useful purpose at all.

Spelling [when you have a single vowel followed by a single consonant at the end of a word, then double the final consonant before adding 'ed'].

Full stop should be here.

Useful connective phrase again.

Spelling ['their', meaning 'belonging to the parents'].

Poor ending to the sentence.

Reasonable conclusion, and the paragraph is introduced by a useful 'concluding connective', though I would have liked to see a final reason given to justify the position:
e.g. 'In the end, I cannot see that the reintroduction of the cane would serve any useful purpose at all, for schools ensure that …'

Examiner's comments

The essay is structured logically. The tone is usually appropriate, though not consistently so, and while punctuation is largely accurate, the candidate has quite serious problems with sentence structure at times.
I think, therefore, that a D grade would be appropriate here.

TASK 11

On this page and the next are two further attempts at answering the question (only the first side of the second essay is printed). Read each response carefully, and then outline the **qualities** and **weaknesses** of each.

You should consider:
- content
- organisation
- paragraphing
- tone and use of language
- punctuation and spelling.

Present your views as a series of bullet points in two columns.

<u>Should the cane be reintroduced in British schools?</u>

No I don't think that the cane should be reintroduced to British Schools.

  I remember one day last year when I had to see the head of year 'cos I was supposed to have done somethink wrong in mrs Gethins class I didn't do nothin but I still had to see the head of year. Now what would have happened if the head of year could of caned me well he would of and I hadnt dome nothink. As it was he asked me what id done and I told him I hadnt done nothink so he said that I must of done somethink so I told him I had'nt but it was a waist of time because he sent me home but at least that was better than the cane. My dad was caned in school lots of times. Once he was caned cos he got to school to early. Have you ever heard of anythink so stupid as caning someone for getting to school early. i'm late most days and I don't get caned. If I did i wouldent come at all. Who would if they were going to get caned when they got there.

  So I don't think the cane should be reintroduced to British Schools.

Should the cane be reintroduced in British schools?

I believe there is an argument for reintroducing the cane in British schools.

Some people believe that to inflict such a dreadful punishment on a child is barbaric and brutal, and likely to lead to long-term psychological damage to the child. I strongly dispute these assertions.

The use of the cane would not be an uncontrolled act of brutality. Rather, it would be reintroduced as a final measure before a pupil's expulsion from school. I believe that it should only be administered with a parent's permission, and should be carried out calmly only by the headteacher of the school, or by a single teacher designated by the headteacher to carry out such a punishment.

In this way, both the pupil conserned and his parents would clearly understand why the punishment was being carried out, and this would be likely, therefore, to change the pupil's behaviour in future. Another significant benefit would be that it takes expulsion, or suspension from school, one step further away, and surely one of the most damaging things that one can do to a child is to deny him his entitlement to education, something that expulsion obviously does.

Regarding the idea that the cane brings about long-term psychological damage, I would give my father as an example to dispute this point. When he was at school, the cane was used from time to time, and he was caned on two occasions: once for smoking, and once for failing to attend a detention. He tells me that on both occasions, he fully accepted that he was in the wrong, and felt no antagonism towards the teacher who had to carry out the caning. Also, he felt that he did change his behaviour as a result of this brief, painful, but in the long run, harmless, punishment.

It could, of course, be argued that if the cane was reintroduced, this would suggest to some pupils that violence was sometimes acceptable.

Again I feel that it is nonsense to suggest that the use of the cane in the controlled way suggested above is 'violent' ...

TASK 11

Printed below are five essay titles. Choose one, and write the essay. You should aim to write about 2–4 sides.

REMEMBER

- **research** your title: you can find information in books, encyclopaedias, on CD-ROMs, on the Internet, in newspapers and magazines, in leaflets and so on
- **gather** your material, and **plan** your essay carefully
- **decide** on your viewpoint, and express this viewpoint as the opening paragraph of your essay
- **use** the main idea/supporting details structure
- **use** appropriate formal language
- **use** connectives to help you to shape your work
- **take care**. Paragraph your work, and write as accurately as you can.

- Should we try to prevent people from taking motor cars into city centres?
- Should sportsmen and women have the right to earn so much money from professional sport?
- How would you go about reducing crime in Britain today?
- Should blood sports be banned?
- In your opinion, what makes 'a good school'?